Hunters' Heritage

A History of Hunting in Michigan

by Eugene T. Petersen

Art Director • Ben Graham

Front cover painting • "Claiming the Shot"
by John George Brown, 1865.
Founders Society Purchase (73.226),
Robert H. Tannahill Foundation Fund.
Courtesy of The Detroit Institute of Arts.

Back cover painting • "Steady Now"
by Gustave Muss-Arnolt.
Courtesy of The Hagley Museum.

MUCC

Published by
Michigan United Conservation Clubs
Box 30235, Lansing, Mich. 48909

*To my Friends
and Sportsmen
on Mackinac Island*

©Copyright 1979 by the Michigan United Conservation Clubs
All rights reserved.
ISBN 0-933112-01-7

PREFACE

The history of hunting and the use of wildlife has long interested me. Not because I am a hunter, for I am not, but because the subject is an integral part of the broader story of wildlife conservation. Anyone who studies that subject soon realizes that the hunters and other sportsmen played a major contributing role in formulating the principles that govern our wildlife program today. Unfortunately, that role is frequently obscured in the emotional debates on the killing of animals.

If we believe in the conservation of wildlife for whatever purpose, we must know what trails our forebears blazed to take us where we are today. The purpose of this study is to attempt to throw some light on the circumstances and attitudes which influenced them.

Eugene T. Petersen
Mackinac Island, 1979

Hunter scores on ducks with flintlock in this 1740 wood cut.

Hunters' Heritage

One June day in 1834, Henry Schoolcraft, United States Indian agent on Mackinac Island, doled out the allotted annuities to a group of bedraggled Chippewas. That night he wrote in his diary, "It is remarkable what straits and sufferings these people undergo each winter for bare existence. They struggle against cold and hunger and are grateful for the least relief."

How was it possible for these northern Michigan Indians to go hungry? They were the world's best hunters. For thousands of years their ancestors had fished and netted whitefish and sturgeon in the Great Lakes, had stalked elk and deer in the forests and trapped and killed beaver and muskrats in the inland lakes and rivers. And for the 200 years white men had been in their midst, the Indians had supplied them with fur-bearing animals in such quantity that pelts were by far the most important New World export to Europe.

Was it because Michigan's wildlife resources were all gone? In 1834, the United States was barely a half century old, and Michigan was not yet a state. Settlements in the territory were almost entirely restricted to the Detroit-Kalamazoo axis, with the vast wildlife-rich interior virtually unknown except to the Indians themselves. By the time America celebrated its centennial in 1876, market hunters were killing 70,000 deer and untold numbers of birds annually for the commercial markets of eastern cities. And in the bicentennial, 1976, an army of sports hunters would take to the marshes, cornfields and forests, to harvest thousands of ducks, geese, pheasants, grouse and deer. No, there was plenty of wildlife left in 1834.

The answer to the paradox of Indian hunger in a land with plenty of edible wildlife lies in the history of hunting and particularly in the changing attitude toward the use of the state's wildlife resources. For most of our history, wild animals were essential for sustenance. They were hunted and killed for food and clothing by individuals for the family unit. However, when fur-bearing animals, especially beaver, developed a commercial value for European markets, the Indians' traditional methods of hunting were changed. They became only fur gatherers, the process of which forced them into the white man's culture and eventually, for many, into wards of the state.

By the 1870s, coinciding with the unrestricted assault on other natural resources and with the growth of urban areas, wildlife, especially deer, pigeons and waterfowl, were killed without restraint by professional market hunters. The best use for the wild animals, it was generally believed, was to supplement or replace the food and fiber provided by domestically raised animals. But a few saw another use for wildlife in the 1870s. A handful of individuals whose recreation was sport hunting challenged the commercial market hunters and demanded enactment of the first state conservation laws to insure a continuing supply of game—and a continuance of their sport. In the 1880s and 90s, the conservation movement under the sportsmen's stimulus took more sophisticated turns with emphasis on enforcement of game laws, habitat improvement, private hunting preserves and experimentation with introduction of non-native species.

Today, a hundred years after the first conservation laws and the end of commercial use of wildlife, hunting in Michigan is one of the most popular participation sports. The hundreds of thousands of hunters who get out of the house and into the marshes, fields and woods are following in the footsteps of countless others who preceded them in the historical past.

In the three or four million years of man's occupation of the world, the settlement of Michigan has been very recent. Most of the time when prehistoric man elsewhere was perfecting his hunting techniques so that he could move more than a few hundred feet from his cave, Michigan was buried under miles of solid ice. It was only after the retreat of the last polar ice glacier 12,000 years ago that men first ventured into these peninsulas. Most anthropologists believe they crossed from Asia via the Bering Straits and Alaska and eventually made their way to the game-rich Great Lakes area.

Culturally, these people did not progress much beyond the stone age until Europeans moved into Michigan in the early 1600s. At a time when the Mayas and Aztecs of Mexico were building pyramids, inventing the calendar and making exquisite gold and silver jewelry, prehistoric Michigan men were producing only a few rock paintings and burial mounds. They hunted with crude stone axes and copper arrow

1

points, but they survived and passed on their knowledge to the Europeans who adopted many of their techniques. Prof. Sherwood Washburn, in a 1965 symposium at the University of Chicago on "Man the Hunter," estimated that agriculture has been important only in the past 2,000 years and that man has hunted for survival during 99 percent of his earthly existence. In the 12,000 years man has lived in Michigan, he hunted and consumed wildlife to keep alive in all but the past 200.

What we know about these prehistoric hunters must be pieced together from sketchy sources. In the 1830s, Schoolcraft recorded legends passed down from generation to generation from northern Michigan Indians for his monumental "History of the Indian Tribes of the United States." Archaeologists digging in old villages and on hunting and fishing sites supply additional data based on recovered artifacts. Most detailed descriptions, however, come from the first Europeans who observed these aboriginal Indians in their native habitat and who were literate enough to describe their customs.

When the French first penetrated North America via the Great Lakes, they found five principal Indian tribes in Michigan, called the Huron, Miami, Potawatomi, Ottawa and Chippewa. Hurons were offshoots of the Iroquois nation, centered in New York State, but had recently been driven by their brothers in bloody battles as far west as Michigan. In the mid-1600s, they lived mainly in Ontario, but a few bands shared southern lower Michigan with the Potawatomi and Miami. The Ottawa and Chippewa, on the other hand, ranged through the north with concentrations near the Straits of Mackinac. All but the Huron were Algonquin stock, which stretched from eastern Canada to the Dakotas.

While some tribes in the south, particularly the Huron, cultivated the soil and practiced farming, all relied on wildlife and fish for sustenance. The Michigan Indian was primarily a hunter who made his home in the thick spruce and pine forests of the north or the hardwoods of the south. Depending on the season, he pitched his tepee near the rivers flowing into the Great Lakes or on the shores of a quiet stream. Highly mobile in his quest for food, he invented and used the fragile birch bark canoe to move amazing distances on the great waterways. Moose, elk, deer and bear were the large game he hunted in the fall and winter, while some buffalo were killed in southern Michigan. The mastodon and mammoth, huge elephant-like creatures, were already extinct by 1600, but when they flourished, they offered a fearful challenge to any hunter.

His weapons were crude. Mostly he used spears and bows and arrows with points laboriously chipped out of flint and affixed with leather thongs. Archaeologists have found literally thousands of these points throughout the state and have even found "factory" sites where they were made. When the hunters discovered copper outcroppings on Isle Royale in Lake Superior, they soon fashioned arrow and spear points out of that metal. Although both stone and copper were made in various sizes and shapes, over 10,000 years of hunting brought no significant change in these basic hunting weapons.

What the Woodland Indian lacked in weaponry, he made up in resourcefulness: he learned the habits of wildlife. No forest creature was more feared than the bear, but his meat was nutritious and the grease highly prized for body decoration. A hibernating bear was aroused from slumber by pounding on the base of his hollow tree, and when he stuck out his head to investigate, he was attacked with spears, knives and clubs. Another favorite method of hunting bear was the deadfall. Indians tied a bait to a huge overhanging log, and when the bear

Bow and arrow was Indians' basic hunting weapon, as shown in drawing below from Sir Francis Drake's "Journal of a Voyage," published in 1586. Hunting techniques included deadfall (inset, right). Indians used snowshoes to great advantage over helplessly mired buffaloes in midwinter.

took it, the falling log struck him and, it was hoped, broke his back. Elk, moose and deer were difficult to kill, so they were hunted in winter when the snow disabled the animals. Alexander Henry, an English fur trader who accompanied such a winter hunting party, described it as follows:

"The stag is very successfully hunted, his feet breaking through at any step, and the crust upon the snow, cutting his legs with its sharp edges, to the very bone. He is consequently in this distress an easy prey, and it frequently happened that we killed twelve in the short space of two hours."

LaHonton, an early French observer, reported that Indians drove nine-foot stakes into the ground, funneling them to a point. These were set along the animal's runway, and deer were driven between them by imitating the cry of a wolf. The funnel terminated in a lake, where the deer were easily clubbed to death. Schoolcraft said that Chippewas hunted deer at night by canoe, using a torch. They made a shield by peeling off a five- to six-foot strip of cedar or elm bark, turning it inside out and painting it black with charcoal. One Indian sat behind this shield in the bow and held a lighted torch made of rolls of tightly wound birch bark poked through a small opening. Deer are strangely transfixed by a light, and the canoe could move close enough for a fellow hunter in the stern to make the kill. Shining is, of course, illegal today.

Small animals were usually found throughout Michigan forests and in the streams. The snowshoe hare, raccoon and squirrel were easily taken with snares. Muskrats were speared in their houses. Otter were captured in a box-like trap that sprung when the animal took an attached fish bait. Highly useful beaver could be killed after destroying their dams and houses. Henry said the Indians drifted downstream silently in their canoes until they came alongside a swimming beaver, then clubbed it to death. Beaver tails were considered especially tasty morsels.

If the Indians were accomplished hunters, they were also good fishermen. According to Chippewa legend, their chief god, Michipaux, who lived on Mackinac Island, guided his people to the Straits of Mackinac, where whitfish, trout and sturgeon abounded. Mackinac is the word for turtle, so named by the Indians because the high-bluffed island resembled that reptile. They had been coming to the Straits for generations to spear and net, and many early French maps show their fishing grounds off the shoals and in the deep water between St. Ignace and the island. Archaeologists frequently find animal-bone harpoons, fish hooks and net-weighting stones while digging on local village sites.

Because hunting was so important a part of Indian life, animals took on a spiritual and religious significance. Prehistoric Indian stone pipes feature effigies of bear, deer and small animals. Young male children were expected to chip out their own stone arrowheads, and their first killed squirrel or bird was the occasion of an elaborate feasting to which the tribe's elders were invited. Henry reported the Indians' idea of after life was to reside in a country "abounding with deer and other animals," but those who had neglected their earthly responsibilities were doomed to travel a barren land, condemned to fighting off gnats "as large as pigeons."

But in this world the game and fish were not always plentiful, and starvation was not unknown. Cycles of abundance were followed by unexplained shortages. Severe winter storms sometimes drove the usually plentiful deer into remote parts of the forest that were inaccessible even to natives on snowshoes. Henry saw a cave where an Indian who could find no other food had killed and eaten a member of his family.

Winter Indian hunting camp is depicted in 19th century drawing at right. Indians used native moose call and European rifle (far right) in hunting moose.

Indians fished with bow and arrow (left) as well as with hook and line. Moose were often hunted at night by attracting them with a lighted bough.

Unwary deer were approached by Indians who concealed themselves under deer hides.

Today, we accept the conservation of wildlife as necessary to preserve species from extinction. The romantic notion is advanced by some writers that the prehistoric Indian was basically a conservator who, in contrast to the European, wisely understood the relationship between unnecessary killing and use. There is no great evidence to support this. His attitude toward wildlife was simple and fundamental. Nature had put the animals in his environment, and he killed them as necessary to survive. Long-range concepts of preservation or even restraint in killing were unknown to him. But because he had only crude stone-age weapons, he was never a threat to the supply of fish and game. When a temporary scarcity occurred, the nomadic Indian simply moved on to a more promising hunting ground. But this all changed in the 17th century.

Sometime about 1622, Etienne Brule and a couple of other Frenchmen paddled their canoe out of eastern Canada into the Ottawa River, then into Georgian Bay and up the St. Marys River to Lake Superior. Along a bank somewhere stood a Chippewa hunter, holding a bow and a stone-tipped arrow while his squaw cooked some strips of venison over an open fire. History does not record what Brule and the Indian said to each other, and it is not likely they reflected long on the symbolic significance. But at that moment, prehistory ended and the historic age began. For better or worse, life would never be the same. Before long the Indian would be holding a flintlock musket, and the squaw would do her cooking in a copper pot.

In the historic march of western civilization, it was inevitable that Europeans would appear in the stone age society of Michigan. But the early 1622 date is surprising when you consider at that time England was still trying to keep alive her first two small settlements of Jamestown and Plymouth on the Atlantic Coast. While it never became a mass transportation system, the St. Lawrence and Great Lakes waterways penetrating westward from the Atlantic made it possible for France to stake her claim deep in the vast interior of the North American continent. In time, the land would produce iron, copper, lumber and a host of other natural resources, but for the first 200 years, there was only one resource that really mattered: fur. Hunting in Michigan changed from killing for sustenance to killing for trade. Calico, colored beads, scissors, guns and brandy flowed west; deer, bear, muskrat, mink and beaver pelts flowed east.

For some time, the French were content to maintain a tenuous long-range trade with the Michigan Indians from their bases in eastern Canada, but in the late 1660s, they were forced to fortify the strategic connecting waterways in the Upper Great Lakes. First they established a post at the eastern end of Lake Superior and the St. Marys River at Sault Ste. Marie, then at the Mackinac Straits between Lakes Huron and Michigan and finally, in 1701, at the western end of Lake Erie at a place they simply called the straits, or Detroit. Their unwavering objective was to set up an exclusive trading system with the local Indians.

Of the three posts, Michilimackinac at the Straits of Mackinac was the most important fur depot during the French era. Typical of French outposts on the frontier, its 300-foot sides were made of 12-foot high cedar pickets. A small bastion jutted out from each corner, and on its raised platform soldiers had mounted a small brass cannon. The water gate entrance was near a small dock used for unloading trade goods from Montreal and furs from Indian hunting camps.

Within the stockade the small French community lived and worked. *Inhabitant*'s cottages of natural posts chinked with clay contrasted with the more impressive squared-timber military, religious and wealthy fur traders' structures. Transplanted peasant farmers from the Old World worked their garden plots while the more skilled artisans, such as coopers and blacksmiths, made shipping barrels and repaired guns and ironware. Their lifeline to Montreal and Quebec was the fleet of supply canoes that made regular trips via the Ottawa River and lower Great Lakes.

Despite a fairly reliable supply route east, the French transplants were never furnished their entire foodstuff needs. They were expected to farm the land, fish the rivers and lakes and take advantage of the bountiful wildlife. They soon became remarkably self-sufficient, not because of their own energy, but rather as a result of help from the local Chippewas and Ottawas. Bear, moose and venison were delivered to the small garrison throughout the winter when the Indians had enough to spare. As soon as migratory waterfowl returned north in the spring and ice left the Straits, canoes filled with ducks, geese and passenger pigeons appeared at the small dock. Beaver flesh, particularly the tail, was an Indian

In this old New York State woodcut, the importance of the western trade in beaver skins is obvious.

delicacy that the Europeans fully appreciated. Peter Kalm, a Swedish visitor who toured Canada in 1750, reported that the fur-bearing creature could even be eaten on fast days because the Pope classified beaver as a fish since it spent so much of its time in the water.

This reliance on Indian game prompted visitors to the French trading communities to remark upon the laziness and lack of ingenuity of the white residents. Lotbiniere, the French engineer who inspected the fortification at Michilimackinac in 1749, reported that although the French were originally farmers, they chose to walk around the fort most of the day gossiping and smoking their pipes or going down to the water to await the Indians bringing in food. "They preferred living on corn, fish and deer or moose grease rather than take the least pain to better their lives."

Charles Cleland, Michigan State University archaeologist who identified and compared bones found at a nearby prehistoric site with those from a French family's garbage dump at Michilimackinac, confirmed this reliance on wild game and fish. He found a greater variety of animals on the French

Bear were delivered to the small garrison at Michilimackinac, along with moose and venison, throughout the winter whenever the Indians had enough to spare.

Leonard Lee Rue III

William B. Mershon used this hunting equipment in the 1860s. The 16-gauge percussion cap doubled-barreled shotgun was made in Scotland. Powder flasks contained gunpowder and shot. The game bag was large enough for nearly a dozen game birds. (From "Recollections of My Fifty Years Hunting and Fishing.")

site, and the Europeans depended on wild game for food more than on their edible domestic animals. Dr. Cleland also concluded much more waterfowl was eaten by the French than by prehistoric Indians, a circumstance he attributed to the introduction of firearms. And indeed many of the bird bones show evidence of shot holes. "The Indian trade was probably the major food source, and the value of such trade was no doubt partially the result of kin ties with the local population," Dr. Cleland wrote.

The fur trade was governed by Montreal authorities through the licensing system. These licenses were sold or awarded to favorites and authorized the recipients to send a canoe of trade goods into the Indian country and bring out a load of furs. Originally the bargaining took place at such a depot as Michilimackinac, but soon it became customary for Frenchmen to accompany Indians to their hunting grounds, spend the winter in their lodges and return with them to the fort early in the spring. Opportunities for great profits led many woodsmen to ignore the license system and trade clandestinely with the indifferent Indians.

As the European demand for pelts grew, so also did the efficiency with which wildlife was hunted. Of all the French cultural innovations thrust upon the primitive Indians, the introduction of the trade gun was the most important in bringing them into the modern age. Although firearms had been known and perfected by Europeans for hundreds of years, it was not until the early 1700s that the Indians obtained this weapon, originally, most historians believe, through Dutch traders in upper New York.

The gun had a 30- to 42-inch barrel of .58 caliber with a deep trigger guard. Locks and flash pans varied somewhat over the years, but invariably the side plate had a distinctive serpentine design. These dragon-like parts are frequently found by archaeologists on trading post sites, and legend has it the natives refused muskets with other designs. Variously called the Mackinac, Northwest or Hudson's Bay gun, depending on where it was traded, the weapon was sturdy and cheap and was manufactured in tremendous quantities. According to Harold Peterson, a leading authority on American historic weapons, the Indian owners cherished the trade musket above all, frequently decorating it with brass tinkling cones or scalps, modifying it to suit their individual needs and doing everything "but take care of it."

Of course, the gun was far superior to traditional hunting methods of trapping, snaring, deadfall, bow and arrow. The Indian quickly mastered its potential as few whites did. For the first time, the odds were definitely on his side in hunting wildlife. Now he combined the hunting prowess of his ancestors with his new firepower. Peter Kalm observed Indians who tied the head of a deer on the back of their own and crept along the ground making animal sounds until they got within range of an inquisitive deer, then shot it.

With ruthless efficiency, the Indians assaulted wildlife to satisfy the insatiable appetite of Europeans for fur. What formerly had been an "as necessary" pursuit for food and shelter became a wholly absorbing occupation. Thousands of pelts from fur-bearing animals moved from Midwest hunting camps by canoe to the great depots, such as Michilimackinac and Detroit, there to be sorted and baled and eventually fed into the mainstream of commerce bound for Montreal and Europe. With this onslaught it was inevitable that hunters had to push even farther west as species such as the beaver simply disappeared from the once-bountiful lakes and streams. Kalm reported in 1750 that beaver were never seen near Montreal, although at one time they had been very plentiful.

The enormous amount of fur that moved through Michilimackinac yearly represented the Indian's productive labor, other than what he needed for his own subsistence. He became a freelance employee of the French merchants, hunting the wildlife resources of Michigan. He produced the fur and, in return, demanded the products of 18th century European culture. As frequently happens, the exchange was uneven, and the French trader profited greatly in dealing with these unsophisticated people. Kalm repeated a widely known story about early traders swapping a large stack of beaver pelts for three times the amount of cinnabar, a cheap body coloring, that would lie on the tip of a knife.

Light blue cloth obtained by the Indian in trade was used for shirts and leggings, with red ribbons to brighten them. Glass beads in a multitude of colors were sewed to the cloth, and bits of procelain were made into wampum belts that had both a religious and superstitious significance. The miraculous change brought about by all this "finery" could be captured in looking glasses, which were always a favorite product.

We will never know how many pelts that were traded for alcohol went to European processing centers. To many Indians, French brandy and English rum held a fascination that amazed even the hard-drinking Europeans. "Nothing," reported Kalm in 1750, "is so dear to them that they would not give away for liquor." He went on to say, "In Canada it is said that if an Indian saw brandy before him and a proposition were made to him to receive a good drink under the condition that he was to be killed thereafter, he might well reflect a little thereupon before giving his consent." It was not unusual for some natives to travel two or three hundred miles with their fur, which had taken all winter to gather, just for the satisfaction of once becoming drunk.

But whether it was brandy, copper kettles or looking glasses, the Michigan Indians were hooked on the material attractions of European civilization. There was no way they could ever return to the simpler primitive life even if they wanted. Now they had to hunt to pay the price, and the effect was to put considerable pressure on Michigan's wildlife resources, especially the once-plentiful beaver. When the fur resources ran out, the Indians traded their land; and when that was gone, they either were assimilated into the white culture or became wards of the new state. Some, unfortunately, as Grace Lee Nute pointed out in her classic study of the fur trade, "became a degraded shiftless people in comparison with the independent, high-minded race of the fur traders' day."

The French and Indian War was part of a global conflict between France and England. In the New World, it was a struggle to see who could control the lucrative Great Lakes fur trade. When British traders offered better prices to the Indian fur hunters and their countrymen attempted to establish permanent English settlements on the Ohio River, war broke out in 1754.

Although no significant military engagements were fought in Michigan, the fate of the fur trading posts of Detroit and Michilimackinac was at stake. French soldiers and 700 Indians under Charles Langlade, a fur trader of northern Michigan, fought the British in Pennsylvania and in the final battles for Montreal and Quebec. Early French victories were offset by British numerical strength, for in a century and a half France had sent only 80,000 people to Canada and these were spread over a 2,000-mile frontier. When Montreal fell in 1760, the

One of the earliest sport hunting pictures shows the E.C. Nicols party camped along the Au Sable in 1876.

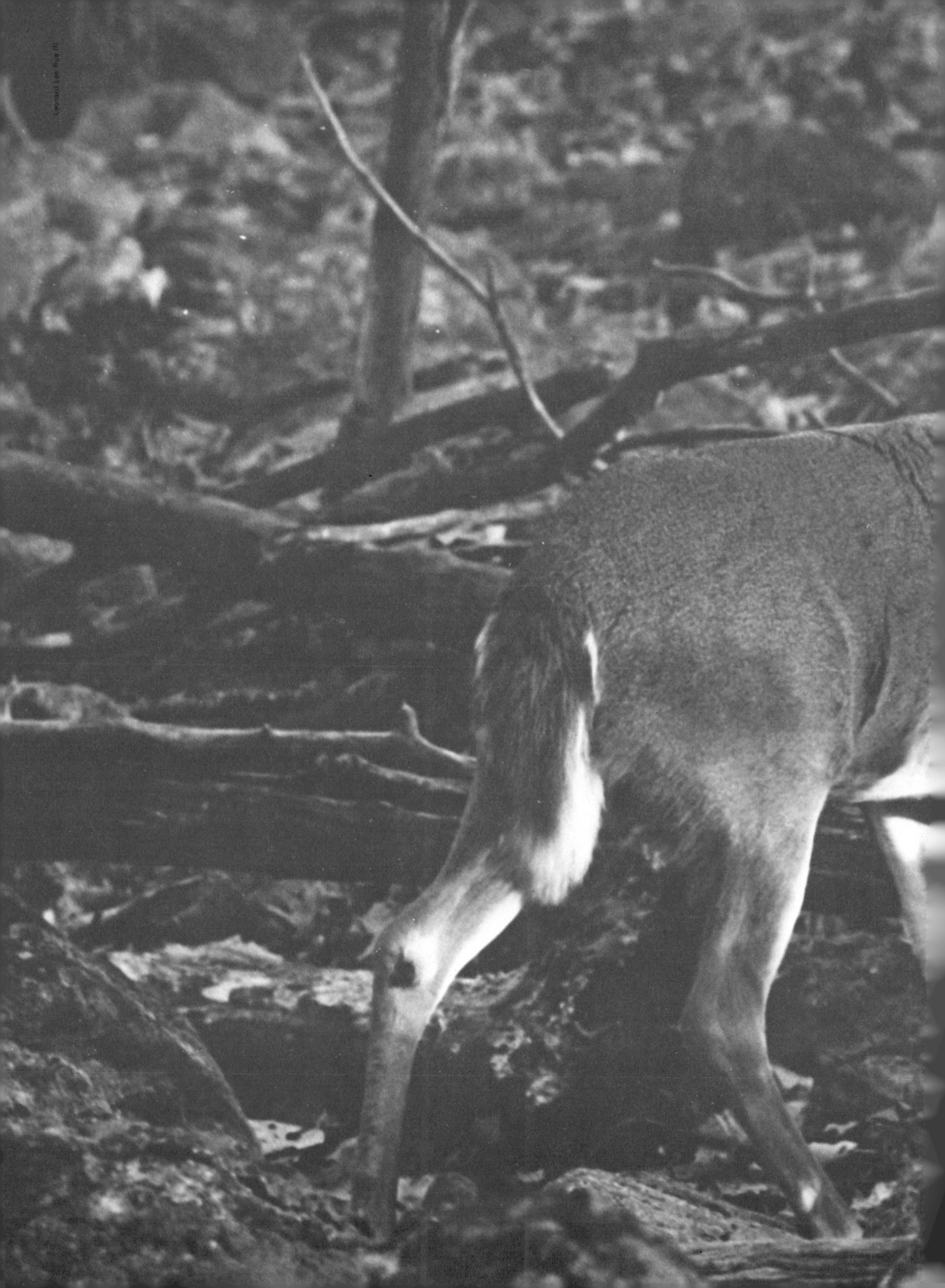

No game species ranks ahead the white-tailed deer among Michigan hunters.

An early sketch of a moccasin-clad, pipe-smoking French hunter who has had a successful pigeon shoot.

war ended quickly and with it France's huge and profitable fur trading enterprise in America.

In Michigan, fighting took a priority over hunting, and the fur trade suffered. Detroit and Michilimackinac were occupied late in 1760, and the realignment of Indian loyalty took place. English fur traders, such as Alexander Henry, Peter Pond and Ezekiel Solomon, soon reestablished the fur gathering network, and the Indians found themselves trading under the British flag.

From 1760 until the Americans took over Michigan in 1796, the British controlled and consolidated the fur trade and thus the whole economy. Gradually, small independent licensed operations that the French had formed were brought together into two large organizations. Over 70 percent of the fur shipped to Europe came through the Hudson's Bay Company or the Northwest Company, which controlled the Great Lakes sources. Most Michigan traders and their Indian hunters shipped their pelts through Michilimackinac to Montreal company warehouses. The value of all British fur imports increased from 16,000 pounds prior to the French and Indian War to over 57,000 pounds when the American Revolution began in 1775, and the Canadian contribution increased from 45 percent to 96 percent. When the war broke out, fur made up 65 percent of all Canadian exports to England.

Beaver made up over half of the exported pelts of major fur-bearing animals. In the summer of 1767, British traders shipped from Michilimackinac the following pelts:

BEAVER	50,938
RACCOON	23,005
MARTEN	9,556
OTTER	5,798
DEER	1,747
FISHER	1,451
FOX	1,340
BEAR	1,142
MINK	807
MUSKRAT	514
WOLF	139
BUFFALO	84
CAT	54

With all this fur going across the ocean, one might think every European would be wearing a fur coat, but such was not the case. In fact, most of the 18th century fur was not used for coats, but for hats. They were made of compressed animal fur or felt. Of all the fur, none compressed better than the short, curly, barbed-end beaver fur found next to the animal's skin. Once compressed, the felt could be cut, shaped and decorated to prevailing fashion. From Charles I in the early 1600s to Queen Victoria in the late 19th century, the beaver hat was the most popular headgear in Europe.

Like the French before them, the British garrison at Michilimackinac depended on Indian-supplied wildlife for sustenance. They welcomed the moose, bear and venison brought in the winter and the waterfowl and passenger pigeons in the spring. Henry noted in the 1760s that these provisions were paid for by the English commander with liquor, and there was no shortage. However, by the 1770s, with large cargo boats operating on the Great Lakes and the disturbances of the American Revolution, Indian-supplied wildlife greatly diminished. In 1779, Major Arendt de Peyster of Michilimackinac complained to Gen. Frederick Haldimand, his superior in Montreal, "As to Indian meat, there are not five carcasses of any kind brought to this fort in the course of a year."

This situation has recently been confirmed by archaeologists digging on the site of the 18th century fort. Thousands of mammal and fish bones from 1740 and 1770 British refuse dumps were analyzed by Dr. Cleland. While he found the French ate much more fish and game than the British, domestic animals, especially cows, sheep and pigs, made up over 75 percent of all the discarded mammal bones of the English period. Cleland attributed this difference in diet to better transportation and concluded: "The French could not count on a supply of pork and beef, so they hunted wild game, while the British who were assured of a supply of those meats were not required to hunt to such an extent."

What about hunting for the "sport of it" in Michigan? It is true that from the beginning of history there was enjoyment and challenge, even though survival depended on it. In a male-dominated society, it was perhaps no accident that the man did the hunting and the woman stayed home to keep the pot boiling—and to clean the game. But when wildlife was no longer needed for the pot, the enjoyment of the hunt became paramount. We find evidence of this in English letters, diaries and journals from the 1760s and 70s.

Englishmen had sport hunted at home before emigrating to the New World and Michigan. John Askin, who moved in with the soldiers soon after the French left Fort Michilimackinac and finally became wealthy in the fur trade, brought with him not only a brace of holster pistols and an English rifle, but a "Spanish barreled fusil," which was a lightweight flintlock commonly used for hunting. Peter Pond, another fur trader who stopped frequently on his way west, wrote in his 1773 diary in his quaint phonetic spelling that the fort's garrison was "Imployed in Hunting, fishing and fowling." "These woods," he said, "aford Partreages, Hairs, Vensen foxis & Rackcones, sum Wild Pigins." It is in the Porteous Journals, however, that we are treated to the details of a hunting expedition.

John Porteous was another English fur trader who came west from Montreal in 1761. Like Pond, he also kept a journal, but where the former described the places he visited, Porteous told what he did. His weekly entries are spiced with observations on wildlife, especially passenger pigeons. "Pidgeons midling plenty since the 20th," he wrote on June 24, 1765, and "Pidgeons still to be found in the woods," in late August. During that long winter, he longed for spring and shooting again. On the last day of April, 1766, despite a late spring storm, he saw what he was looking for: "Some pidgeons now begin to cross the straits very high toward Gros Cap." The annual migration had begun.

European sportsmen who came to Michigan were accustomed to this kind of hunting in the Old World. Pheasants arise from a private fenced preserve, while servants and game keepers exhort the dogs to retrieve the downed birds.

William B. Mershon, one of Michigan's most illustrious sportsmen, considered the wild turkey to be the grandest game bird of all.

Len Rue Jr.

His entries for the next week tell about a hunting expedition to Waugoshance with Hugh Mitchell, Henry Bostwick, Charles Patterson and Forest Oakes, fellow fur traders from the fort. They set out in a bateau, a large flat-bottomed vessel equipped both with oars and sail, across Cecil Bay to the peninsula that juts out into Lake Michigan about 15 miles southwest of present-day Mackinaw City. It was slow going, and they made their way "with no little difficulty, despite a contrary wind and Mountains of Ice, 30 feet high." Near the peninsula they had to drag their boat over 60 feet of ice to reach shore.

The hunters found the weather bad and the birds scarce. "Frooze last night as the former," he wrote on May 2. On the 3rd, "Very hard frost still," and the fourth day it got worse with "Frost, rain, hail all night and snowed until noon with a cold east wind."

The only birds were some high flying geese, "but no chance at them."

On the 5th, the weather improved somewhat and so did the hunting. With "great labor in water and marshes," they managed to kill a number of Canada geese, plover, sheldrakes and "ducks," which Porteous does not identify further. Either satisfied with their bag, disgusted with the weather or disappointed in failing to find the succulent pigeons, they returned to their boat and with a "moderate breeze aft" reached the fort by noon.

The names of Porteous' hunting party appear only as footnotes in the more significant drama of the American Revolution. Hugh Mitchell is mentioned only once again in the Porteous Journal when the two of them, accompanied by Mitchell's Negro slave, made a hazardous winter ice crossing to Les Cheneaux Islands in northern Lake Huron. Henry Bostwick, who also became one of the most prominent Mackinac traders, already had been captured by the Indians when they took the fort in 1763. Ransomed at Montreal, he returned to the Straits and in 1780 was one of the signatories in the purchase of Mackinac Island from the local Chippewas. Charles Patterson became a founder of the Northwest Fur Company and died in 1788 when his canoe overturned 60 miles west of Fort Michilimackinac at what is now appropriately called Patterson's Point. Forest Oakes was in and out of Mackinac until he died in Montreal in 1783. He will be remembered by posterity not as a sportsman, but as a hard-drinking fur trader who, after a night of frivolity on Nov. 7, 1769, smashed into the post doctor's home and almost killed him. In a formal charge, Dr. Daniel Morison quoted the culprit as saying, "Doctor, doctor, damn your blood. Get up and give us a bowl of toddy, otherwise you'll repent it."

Porteous himself settled in Montreal, where a contemporary called him the "most loyal, sterling and moderate person in the community." A wealthy man, he owned the *Vengeance*, a small privateer that preyed on American colonial shipping during the Revolution.

Michigan stayed firmly under British control during the American Revolution. The political and economic debates that divided Englishmen in the eastern colonies were absent in the western fur trading posts. Furs continued to flow into Michilimackinac without much interruption under the tight controls of the Crown and the Northwest Company. Frenchmen who had stayed to work under the British flag and the Indian hunters remained basically loyal despite considerable wooing from the American rebels. Yet there were distant military reverses.

British Great Lakes transportation routes were unchallenged

John Askin, a prosperous English fur trader at Fort Michilimackinac, included in his 1777 inventory not only an English rifle but the popular sport fusil he used for small game.

seriously by the Colonial army, but the Americans did strike hard at some lesser fur trading posts in the Illinois country. Major George Rogers Clark led a small force of Virginia and Kentucky settlers and won Cahokia and Kaskaskia on the Mississippi and Vincennes in central Indiana. When Col. Henry Hamilton of the Detroit post attempted to help Vincennes, he was promptly captured by Clark and clapped into a Williamsburg prison, where he sat for the duration. Major Patrick Sinclair took command of Fort Michilimackinac and hurriedly moved it to Mackinac Island, where he could better defend the fur center in an expected American assault.

Although Clark was never able to muster an attack on Detroit, much less Michilimackinac, his military success in the Midwest was in part responsible for the boundary between the United States and British Canada being drawn at the Great Lakes rather than the Ohio River in 1783.

However, what the Americans won at the peace table, they were unable to occupy for 13 years. Post-war haggling between the United States and England and considerable pressure on the English court by the Northwest Fur Company resulted in the forts at Detroit and Michilimackinac remaining under the British Ensign until 1796.

The American Revolution had significant implications for hunting and fishing. First, the land no longer belonged to George III but to the new nation to be used by the people for their benefit and enjoyment. Protection of wildlife became the responsibility of the state, and, although serious conservation laws would not come to Michigan for nearly a century, the natural resources of game and fish were as much a part of the nation's heritage as its political institutions. Finally, the new nation inherited the Indians and the problem of their relations with the new white settlers who were about to move into the rich farming lands.

There was another important heritage of the struggle for independence more subtle than those political changes because it had to do with the self-reliant character of the New World people. As every school child knows, the American Revolutionists were ordinary citizens who had to fight well-trained and often mercenary soldiers. The farmers of Virginia, Massachusetts and Pennsylvania were thrown into battles armed with little more than their muskets and a hatred for George III. While not all of them could snuff out a candle at 50 yards, years of hunting experience made them more than a match for the British professionals. This individual effort so natural to people accustomed to depending on their own resources would characterize many who found a new home in Michigan after the war.

The American fur trading era was short and ruthless. The German immigrant, John Jacob Astor, organized the American Fur Company in 1808 with its headquarters on Mackinac Island. Aided by a benevolent Congress that restricted fur trading in the United States to its citizens, Astor had a complete monopoly by 1816. His Mackinac agents built their impressive warehouses and clerks' quarters on Market Street and here received, sorted, cleaned, baled and shipped millions of dollars worth of deer, beaver, mink and muskrat. The word went out to kill every kind of fur-bearing animal, and thousands of hunters, both Indian and white, responded. It may have been the golden age of the Michigan fur trade, but in the words of Ida Johnson, "It was a period of systematic, wholesale exploitation of the furred creatures of her forest by factory fur trading company and independent traders, without thought of reservation or preservation."

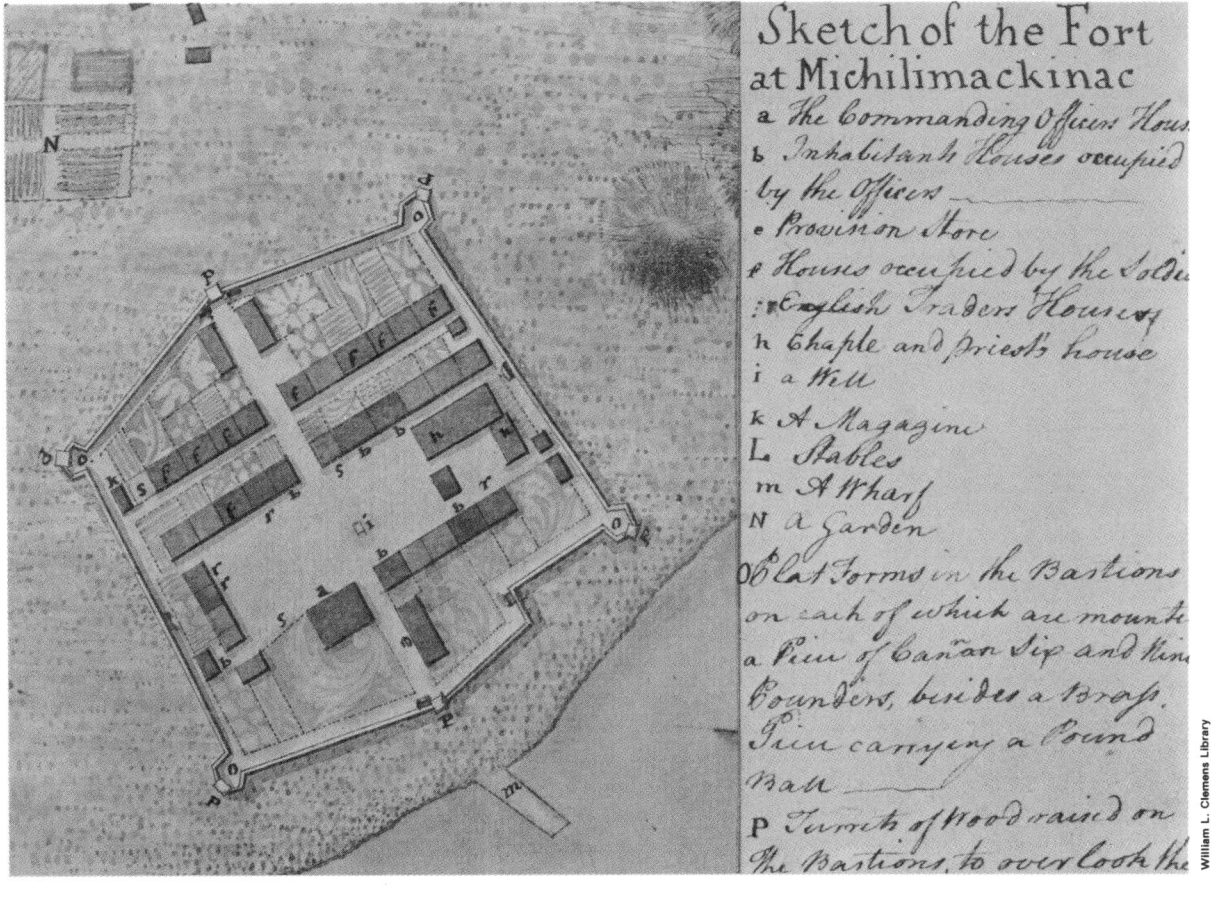

No weapon changed hunting more than the gun. Commonly called the Mackinac or Northwest gun, this firearm usually had a serpentine insignia on the side of the stock. (From "Treasury of the Gun.")

Of course, it could not last. The once plentiful fur resources were greatly depleted. By 1830, Astor saw the handwriting on the wall, sold his Michigan based company and began to build a new fur empire on the West Coast. White hunters moved on to find work in the Upper Peninsula iron and copper mines or on the farms in southern Michigan. Indian hunters drifted into poverty, their means of support gone and lacking the basic self-sufficiency of their ancestors whom the French, 200 years ago, had led down this road of economic slavery.

There is not much left in the state of these two centuries of commercial fur hunting, but what there is you can still see on Mackinac Island. The home of Astor's principal agent, Robert Stuart, dominates the eastern end of Market Street. In it are period furnishings of the 1820s, and you can see the monstrous fur press or examine the entries in aged American Fur Company ledgers. The cavernous Astor warehouse is now the community hall, where, instead of shelves piled high with beaver, you are likely to see the island residents playing bingo.

In the 1830s, a wave of immigrants moved into the Michigan Territory at a rate unknown in American history. In the first decade of the 19th century, only four towns—Mackinac Island, Sault Ste. Marie, Monroe and Detroit—had any sizable population, and Detroit had barely a thousand souls. But in 1836, they were pouring in at a rate of 2,000 a day. Most came from New England or western New York via the Erie Canal, St. Lawrence River and Lower Great Lakes. They paused in Detroit long enough to purchase southern Michigan land at $1.25 an acre and the few essentials of living they had not brought with them. If they were not rich, neither were they poor, for it took some cash to start life anew in a strange land. Most were English, but unlike their older, footloose, fur-trading brethren, these newcomers were farmers and, God willing, they were in Michigan to stay.

The land was fertile and the wildlife abundant. Mostly they sought the prairies or "oak openings," so they did not have literally to carve out their fields in the hardwoods. Game was frequently a nuisance, so the women and children had to keep constant watch during the growing season to frighten squirrels, raccoons, deer, wolves, bear and other marauders away from the young grain. Typical of the new pioneers was the Nowlin family, who staked out their homestead near Dearborn in 1833. Their teenage son Bill, who kept a diary, found wild animals and game numerous. Sometimes the deer came where his father had cut trees and browsed the tops. Occasionally, there were tracks in the yard almost up to the house. Wolves also were common. "We could often hear them at night, first at one point, then answers from another and another direction, until the woods rang with their unearthly yells."

Helping his parents make a living in frontier Michigan left little time for sports, but Bill occasionally found time to hunt: "A small instrument that I almost always carried in my vest pocket . . . was made from the hollow bone of a turkey's wing. I called it a turkey call. By holding the end of my hand and sucking it right, it would make a noise, or squeak, very similar to the turkey's voice . . . I would . . . take the holloe bone out of my pocket and call. I have seen them come up on the run, sometimes one, at other times more. While lying in ambush once, I shot two at the same time with one rifle bullet and got them both."

From 1825 to 1860, these waves of immigrants spread westward through southern lower Michigan, clearing the land before them. Small villages of Ann Arbor, Hillsdale, Albion, Jackson and Kalamazoo were the nucleii of an agricultural economy. When all the fertile lands were taken, they edged north of Saginaw, St. Johns and Ionia. But here they ran into the towering pines, spruce and hemlock and had to wait until the loggers cleared the land in the 1860s and 1870s. As it turned out, the future of northern Michigan was not to be blocks of 160-acre farms, but a vast cutover and burnt landscape of second growth forests that interested the sports-minded hunters and fishermen.

The character of the farmers was conservative, self-reliant and independent. They were hospitable to strangers, but suspicious of outside ideas. Local government they accepted, but distant politics did not interest them. In most cases, they were not concerned with economic or political issues beyond their community. Long working hours and a constant struggle to improve left little time for recreation. Most were not avid hunters. When they did hunt, it was usually for food. Wildlife of the various species, including deer, elk, waterfowl and pigeons, was considered a local resource, and if it could bring cash from commercial market hunters, so much the better. They developed a proprietary attitude toward what they considered their fish and game and would resist any outside attempts to conserve or regulate its use.

In the meantime, the Indians were pushed off the land to make way for the farmers. What some of the more far-sighted chiefs had feared now happened; namely, the clearing and fencing of their land. In a series of seven treaties, the Ottawa, Chippewa and Potawatomi deeded all of Michigan to the government. The treaty concept and subsequent Indian policies assumed the Indians would be absorbed into the agricultural system, but in practice their traditional hunting way of life would end, and the annuities they began to collect from the government were no substitute for the fur trade barter system of the previous century. The future of many of these fur gatherers and their descendants would be poverty and near starvation if they could not be assimilated into the white culture.

The Indian treaties opened the land, not only for farming, but for the unrestrained commercial exploitation of the state's vast lumber resources. From 1860 to 1890, logging companies attacked the hardwood stands in the south and the pine forests in the north with ruthless efficiency to supply wood for the growing urban centers. The railroads which spanned the continent in the 1860s and tied Michigan into the mainstream of American commerce were pushed northward in the 60s and 70s to provide an efficient way to get the logs out of the erstwhile wilderness.

The Flint and Pere Marquette joined Saginaw and Ludington by the mid-1860s. The Ann Arbor Railroad cut diagonally across the state and reached Lake Michigan at Frankfort a short time later. The two principal northern logging lines were the Grand Rapids and Indiana on the west side of the state, which reached Petoskey in 1875 and Mackinaw City in 1882, and the Michigan Central, which rapidly cut through the heart of the state's white pine belt and helped establish such towns as Grayling and Gaylord. It, too, reached the Straits of Mackinac by 1882. The *Pontiac Gazette* made no idle boast when inviting its readers to "come out and watch the forest move back before your very eyes."

The opening of the north in the 1870s brought an era of commercial hunting similar to the onslaught on fur-bearing animals in the 17th and 18th centuries. This time, it was not fur that lured the hunters, but the edible wildlife. Deer and passenger pigeons not only supplemented the camp food of

In mid-19th century Currier and Ives painting (top), hunter waits in his blind for passenger pigeons to come within range. Adult male pigeon is pictured at left.

logging and railroad dining halls, but were shipped south and east to the urban areas to be sold in produce markets alongside cattle, hogs and vegetables. It was the era of market hunting, most of which was done by Civil War sharpshooting veterans who found both employment and adventure in practicing their skills.

In the 1870s, no one paid much attention to the systematic killing of wildlife for food by the market hunters. The north was a vast forest, largely unknown, unvisited, with a limitless reservoir of wildlife. The wild animals and birds were a natural resource to be consumed like any other, and the best use of them was for food. They belonged to everybody and therefore to nobody. Yet as the slaughter went on, a few voices were raised in protest. Those came from the sportsmen who saw the folly of killing wildlife for the insatiable pot when, with a little conservation, the birds and animals could provide sport and recreation for generations of hunters.

Hunting for sport is probably as old as the first encounter between animal and man. While it is difficult to separate the killing of wild animals for sustenance or simply for fun, by the early 1870s in Michigan, a small number of citizens, who followed in the footsteps of Porteous and his party a century earlier, were afield primarily for recreation. By then, the state was changing from predominantly rural agricultural society to industry and urbanization. If Saginaw and Bay City were the lumbering centers of the state, Grand Rapids was fast becoming the furniture-making capitol. Flint had thriving wagon-manufacturing plants, and Detroit was producing locomotives for the growing railroad network. This industrialization brought wealth and leisure to increasing numbers of people and, with it, the opportunity to hunt and fish for sport.

This is not to say that hunting became the hobby of the masses overnight. That had to wait for a generation or more, but for those who could afford it, hunting became a very popular pastime. Sportsmen formed clubs in the early 1870s, such as the Morenci Club of Mt. Clemens, Baw-ko-Tung of Bay City, Lake St. Clair Fishing and Shooting Club and the Wolverine Club of Flint. These were primarily social organizations that sponsored hunting trips, shooting matches and dog field training sessions. Occasionally, members or guests read papers on birds and animals, but mainly the clubs offered receptive audiences for endless tales of hunting and angling exploits.

William B. Mershon, who published his recollections of hunting in the Saginaw area in 1923, recalled his sport hunting activities in the 1880s. Many March mornings he shot pigeons near his house as they made their daily flights to feeding grounds. It was "no trick to get 75 or 100 birds before breakfast." Jacksnipe hunting was always good near bogs covered with marsh hay. Woodcock hunting began every July 5 because "we had to have something to shoot at and besides you couldn't find them in August." Golden plover were plentiful around Saginaw, and Mershon thought them the most delicious to eat of all the game birds. Near Flint he shot quail almost at will, although he remembered some years when he did not see any.

Ruffed grouse was a good game bird, but the grandest of all, he believed, was the turkey. He and his father hunted them along the edges of farmers' fields where the birds came out of the hardwood forests to feed on buckwheat. Rarely did they fly into the trees, and noise never bothered them, but they were wary and had good eyesight, so the trick was to track them in the snow and get close enough for a shot. In the 80s, it became harder to find them, and when Mershon shot one in 1886, he had the 2¾-pound bird mounted and called him the "last of his race."

The Grand Rapids & Indiana Railroad was pledged "to make sportsmen feel at home" on its line. Railroads made it possible for sportsmen to travel to distant parts of the state, like the Sturgeon River country in Dickinson County where the E. C. Nicols party from Jackson is shown at its hunting camp in the 1886 photograph below.

The Michigan Historical Collection of the University of Michigan

Edward Nicols of Jackson recollected deer hunting trips close to home with his friends in the 1860s. He and his father would hitch up a team to a farm wagon, load it with a large canvas tent, cooking utensils, blankets and a small supply of groceries, which they intended to supplement with fish and venison, and head out of town. Each hunter carried a muzzle loading rifle with pouches of ball, patches and powder, a weapon, Nicols recalled, that "gave him but one chance at a deer and this required steady nerve, accurate eye, and delicate trigger finger." The party also included several hounds used to track wounded deer and "to stir them up in the morning."

Michigan hunters of the 1870s were not particularly diligent about sharing their experiences with posterity. In trying to reconstruct sport hunting, we are forced to rely upon an occasional reminiscence by a Mershon or Nicols, newspaper accounts of an unusual hunt, sketches, an early photograph or stories by professional writers who had firsthand experiences in Michigan hunting camps. For the most part, these articles appeared in popular journals of the day, such as *American Field, Forest and Stream* and *Scribner's*. One such account that appeared in the April 1878 issue of the latter was written by McKay Laffan, a New York sportsman who had been invited to join a deer hunting party on the Au Sable River in the fall of 1877.

The New Yorker's story is significant for several reasons. In the first place, he looks upon the north woods and local hunter accommodations from an outside point of view and so provides interesting details of the famed Au Sable hunting grounds at the height of the lumbering era. Secondly, he describes how an 1877 sportsman camped, hunted and killed deer. Finally, we get a pretty good picture of the inter-relationship of local farmers and loggers with the visiting sportsmen.

The Easterner began his story at a Bay City steamer dock, where he joined 11 other hunters from Michigan early in October. The plan was to take a small coastal lake boat up Saginaw Bay to Tawas and then be transported by wagon to a campsite on the main branch of the Au Sable.

On the wharf all was confusion. Introductions and pleasantries were shouted over a chorus of howling and yelping hunting dogs that included not only a dozen from the Laffan group, but many others from deer hunting parties that were bound for various camps north and south of Tawas. They shared the deck with these sportsmen, with farmers returning home after shopping in Bay City and with tough-looking woodsmen heading for the numerous inland lumber camps that were marked only by docks occasionally stretching out from the wilderness shore.

"We had a delightful run up Saginaw Bay," he wrote. The sun set after a perfect day in a glorious display of color in the western sky, and their enthusiasm was dampened only slightly when the captain sourly predicted that tomorrow it would "rain like blazes."

At 8:30 p.m., they bumped against the dock at East Tawas, where Curtis, their local guide, greeted them cheerily in the evening darkness and helped load their equipment and dogs on his stout wagon. After a half-hour ride, they reached an inn, where they bedded down for the night, but not until their enormously fat host had served a delicious supper of broiled venison from a deer he had shot that very day.

Early next morning, they left Tawas in two wagons. Nine of the hunters rode in the lead, while Curtis and his son followed with the luggage. Three of the hunters walked behind and, although they could take turns in the wagon, apparently did not mind making the 25-mile journey on foot.

George Shiras III © National Geographic Society

The Peter White hunting camp in Alger County in the Upper Peninsula about 1900.

Perhaps they walked to keep warm or to take their minds off the foul weather. As the captain had predicted, it rained in a steady downpour. For a while, the novelty of passing through the scrub oak, tall Norway pine, glistening white birch and nearly impenetrable tangles of undergrowth interested Laffan, but the steady cold rain on his face put out his cigar, chilled him to the bone and plunged him into a miserable frame of mind. A corduroy road through a swamp jarred every bone in his body, and, where the surface logs were gone, the wagon rocked, swayed and splashed through a series of mudholes. Finally, they reached a higher ground with firm sand, and the horses moved ahead at a quieter pace.

Sometime recently, a fire had swept across the sand plateau, and they drove for miles through the charred tree trunks, called "burnings," where "great lofty pines, whose stems are blackened from the root to as high as the fire had reached, huge, distorted and disfigured stand gloomily among their moldering brethren extending their dead and broken arms in mute testimony of lost grace and beauty."

After they set up camp, some of the sportsmen made a 15-minute walk through the "burnings" to the Au Sable River.

Early in the afternoon, the wagons came over a small rise, and below them lay the prosperous-looking Thompson farm, where Curtis had arranged for them to spend the night. Thompson proved to be a hale and hearty backwoodsman who owned thousands of acres of pine which his loggers were getting out to the mill. Mrs. Thompson, "a refined lady," prepared a magnificent meal of roast venison, broiled chicken, a sampling of the farm's vegetables and great glass pitchers of milk and cream—all served on a white tablecloth. It was most welcome, but hardly what he expected at the end of a 25-mile corduroy road deep in the woods.

That evening, the sportsmen had a chance to mingle with Thompson's loggers. The visitor found them mostly French Canadians, loud and good-humored. They talked about logging problems, especially the absence of snow for the large sleighs, and punctuated their opinions with considerable profanity which was "startling in its originality, redundancy and obscurity of purpose." Later their host told them that, when the loggers were paid at the end of the season, they went to the lake settlements, got drunk for weeks at a time and attacked each other with gun and knife in reckless abandon.

The next day, they loaded one of the wagons with their camp gear and followed it on foot for six miles to their final destination, a former lumber camp near a small stream. A rickety barn, former blacksmith shop and a "well-ventilated house" of log construction were all that remained of Camp Erwin, as it was called. William Bamfield and his wife, who lived in a small bedroom in the house, were hired to cook and do chores for the hunters.

After they set up camp, some of the sportsmen made a 15-minute walk through the "burnings" to the Au Sable. At a height of 150 feet they looked down upon the river as it flowed silently through many bends on its way to Lake Huron at Oscoda. Its color Laffan described as "dark brown sherry" and its current as swift and powerful. Despite the desolate burned-over land through which it flowed, the "Sauble" greatly impressed the author. Writing a century ago, he predicted interestingly that it "will always preserve its wildness and its desolation since in the future the wilderness through which it flows will be even wilder and more desolate than now."

That evening, one of the experienced Michigan deer hunters explained how they would hunt the following day. Most of the sportsmen would take separate posts near the river along deer runways, while Curtis and two other hunters would take the dozen dogs, make a wide arc above the river and drive the deer toward the runways. He explained that when the animals are pursued by dogs, they will invariably head for water to elude them, usually using their customary runways, where hunters could shoot them as they swam across the river.

Although Laffan and his party were hunting for deer, through nightly discussions he learned that other species of game were still plentiful in Michigan. The fur-bearing animals, such as beaver, marten, fisher and lynx, had been greatly thinned out by trappers, but bear and wolves were still numerous. Rabbits and ruffed grouse were plentiful, but what elk remained were in the extreme northern part of the peninsula. It was commonly believed Michigan deer were the largest on the continent, with creditable reports of some bucks weighing 250 pounds. The largest shot by Laffan's party were about 225 pounds.

At 4:30 the next morning, Laffan and the others were awakened by Bamfield's loud shout of "Breakfast!" They slowly arose from their hay-filled mattresses and made their way to the first floor. Here Mrs. Bamfield attended her frying pans filled with sizzling rashers of bacon and her pots of hot coffee. After a short trip outside to make their toilet, they sat down to a hearty meal of bacon, boiled potatoes, fried onions, bread and butter with plenty of strong, hot coffee to wash it down. "Coats were buttoned up, rubber blankets and ammunition belts slung over shoulders, cartridge magazines filled, hatchets stuck into belts, rifles shouldered and out we sallied into the darkness through which the faintest glimmer of gray was just showing in the east."

Laffan's assigned post was on the river and not far from camp, but to reach it he had to walk through a low-lying stretch of cedar swamp which flanked both sides of the Au Sable. The thicket of fallen, decayed and live cedars whose moss-covered roots camouflaged water-filled holes made it necessary to choose his path carefully, a challenge not made easier by steadily falling rain and snow. After 200 yards of this,

Successful hunt did nothing to brighten the countenance of the stern-faced hunter in 1880 photograph. In the other photo, an early daguerreotype, a hunter poses stiffly in front of a painted landscape with four stuffed squirrels in the foreground.

he finally reached the river bank near his runway, which fortunately opened on a relatively high sand mound and offered good sighting along the bank.

But if the visibility was good, the exposure to the driving rain was bad, and the Easterner began the first of many hours in an uncomfortable state. His hands were numb, but he was afraid to put on his heavy gloves for fear they would hamper his shooting. His teeth chattered like "miniature castanets." He stamped his feet, did the "London cabman's exercise" with his hands and arms, all the while steadily watching the river and listening for the dogs.

Once, he heard distant shots and barking, but no deer came down his runway. In the early afternoon, young Chris, whose job it was to watch the river and retrieve dead deer as they floated down, poled his boat up to Laffan's runway and told him he'd better come to camp because the dogs and hunters were all in, and one buck and a fawn had been shot.

At camp that night, the lucky hunter had to tell again and again how he saw the big buck swimming across the river and on his second shot hit a vital spot. A few minutes later, he had dispatched the fawn in the same way, and both animals were recovered by young Curtis two miles downstream from his runway. For the 11 other sportsmen, it was "wait until tomorrow," but their disappointment was somewhat lessened by a good meal of venison, cabbage, onions and potatoes. The aroma would do justice to famed Delmonico's, thought Laffan, and "the air of the Sauble would be worth any amount of money in New York."

With high hopes, the Easterner took his same post on the river next morning. Someone had told him there would be nothing wrong with a small fire along the bank, and he happily occupied his day in this task. The smoke blew into his eyes, but he was not troubled with any deer, and at 2:30 in the afternoon, he left for camp, having heard neither shots nor dogs this day.

It was now the sixth day, and although a dozen deer hung in the barn, Laffan had seen not one alive. He passed the tedious hours on his runway debating with himself on the merits of this method of hunting. Suddenly, he heard a splash and looked up to see a large doe swimming across the river. He shouldered his Winchester, took careful aim and shot. The doe went under water but came to the surface just before it rounded a bend. "This performance produced a sense of pleasant inflation. All my fears were dispelled, and I felt a keen desire for the presence of others to whom to impart the agreeable fact."

But Laffan's exuberance was short lived. A few minutes later, Curtis poled his boat up to the runway, and the New Yorker could not believe it when the young man told him he had seen no deer floating down the river. Together, they examined the banks beyond the bend and after finding tracks and a trail of blood, concluded sadly the wounded animal had probably made it into an impenetrable thicket and was beyond reach. So ended day six.

Occasionally, the hunters went out at night to search for a lost dog or for slain deer that might have been caught in a tangle of roots along the river bank as they floated down from the shooting areas. During these operations along the shore, the common method of supplementing the feeble light of their lanterns was to touch a match to the base of a birch tree, which in a minute became a roaring torch of sparking and spectacular flame temporarily lighting the surrounding countryside.

Drawings by McKay Laffan to illustrate his account of an 1877 deer hunting trip along the Au Sable River. From left, the drawings were captioned: Hung Up. A Ton and a Half of Venison. Camp Erwin. Checking the Dogs. A General Surprise.

Hope springs eternal, and the next morning Laffan was again at his post. He peered into the cedar swamp and up and down the river. When he heard gunfire and the baying of dogs downstream, his hopes quickened, but the noise soon died away. Suddenly, "I saw the brush about some cedar roots open, and out there sprang into the shallow water a noble buck. He bore himself proudly as he stood in the water and turned to listen for the bay of the dogs he had outrun."

Laffan slowly raised his rifle, aimed confidently, and when the report sounded, the buck pitched forward into the stream. By the time it floated past Laffan, it was already dead.

This time, young Curtis had no trouble retrieving the deer, and by the time the Eastern sportsman returned to camp later that afternoon, the big buck was already hanging in the barn. After he received the acclamations of his fellow hunters and measurements were taken, his buck was given the place of honor at the head of the line.

Laffan did not kill any more deer, but by the time they broke camp some days later, there were 23 hanging on the pole.

It had been a successful outing in more ways than one. The dogs were brought in a little worse for wear, he thought, but none had been lost.

Laffan's party obviously had the respect of the Au Sable people. They probably paid well for their services, treated the locals with courtesy ("No visitor left camp hungry—or thirsty") and over the years of fall hunting had developed a friendship with the loggers and farmers. But it was not always so with visiting sportsmen, he learned. One party from Bay City, while hunting in the same general area, lost three dogs to strychnine poisoning and had two others shot by the woodsmen as a message they were not welcome. Sometimes the hostility took an even more serious turn, as when some Ohio sportsmen who also had lost their dogs to poisoning retaliated by burning down the barn of a farmer suspect.

In a final note, McKay Laffan recorded that they had arrived safely in Detroit with 2½ tons of venison, said their farewells and went on their individual ways, ending an "expedition with plenty of wholesome recreation to make one's recollection of it wholly pleasant."

But was it an expedition of sportsmen? Was it a fair test, matching the instincts of deer and the skill of the hunter? Is shooting exhausted animals swimming across a river a sporting event? Or was it simply a contrived roundup of deer by highly trained dogs to serve as a test of marksmanship by stationary hunters? There was no criticism in Laffan's party, and indeed the practice of hunting deer with dogs and shooting them in the water was widely accepted in the 1870s.

Yet, when McKay Laffan faced that big buck after a week of physical misery and bad luck, he had a decision to make and not long to make it. The swimming animal would presumably be an easy and safe shot, but "I hesitated a moment, doubtful if I should let him get into the stream and swim down, or shoot at him as he stood. I chose the latter." Perhaps this is the essence of sportsmanship.

By the early 80s, the sportsmen were taking advantage of rail transportation north and vied with lumbermen and market hunters to blaze new trails into the interior. The wagons now brought them only to the nearest railroad station, where they boarded the next local. Baggage cars carried their dogs, tents, cots, stoves and boxes filled with guns, cooking dishes, lanterns and warm clothing. En route, they enjoyed a leisurely meal with cigars and whiskey on the train or dined in the lunchroom at a local station. They telegraphed ahead for guides to meet them at a rail siding and haul them deep into the woods to a promising site. From the local farmers they purchased ice, milk and vegetables. They were still roughing it, but they were "up north," and the comforts of home were not so remote.

Far from resenting having to handle all the paraphernalia of the touring sportsmen, the railroad companies actively solicited this business. Charles Halleck, editor of *Forest and Stream,* acknowledged this in 1877 when he wrote, "Pioneer railroads recognize the value of encouraging sportsmen to visit the regions they penetrate, for sportsmen invariably follow the lumberman and precede the farmer." The Grand Rapids and Indiana Railroad published brochures advertising itself as "The Fishing Line" and promised sportsmen every consideration. They even offered to rent, for $10 a day, railroad camp cars which were equipped with berths, stoves, utensils, tables and ice chests and could be shunted off at a northern rail siding.

Some sportsmen bought their own private camp cars and simply arranged for the railroads to haul them north or west to deer or bird hunting grounds. One of the first of these in Michigan was an old circus car bought at a sheriff's sale at Saginaw in 1883 and remodeled into a hunting car. It had 12 bunks, kitchen, large ice box, storage space and an observation deck on one end. A local sportsmen's club used it mainly on fall deer hunting trips near Harrison. The "William B. Mershon" was built in 1894 for $8,000 and boasted, in addition to the usual cooking and sleeping accommodations, a luxury of a bathroom and tub. Mershon and his party made frequent trips to Grayling and the Au Sable, but they also hunted birds in North Dakota.

The growing interest in sport hunting in Michigan was reflected in newspapers and magazines. The sport columns of the *Detroit Evenings News, Bay City Times* and *Grand Rapids Democrat* reported club meetings, scores of local shooting matches and news notes on successful hunting expeditions. On the national level, the *American Field* and *Forest and Stream* gave expanded coverage to habits of animals, the latest camping gear, new sporting guns, unusual hunting experiences of its readers and staff-written pieces on productive hunting grounds and trout streams. Halleck kept up a lively correspondence with Michigan sportsmen, and in 1876, a month he spent fishing in the Indian and Jordan Rivers was the subject of a series he called "Rambles in Northern Michigan."

Sport hunting also grew in popularity with the rise of the first truly national heroes who demonstrated amazing marksmanship with guns. The first of these was Adam H. Bogardus, a Midwesterner from Illinois who gained his expertise shooting migratory ducks and other waterfowl along the Mississippi flyway for the produce markets of Chicago. Tall, powerfully rugged, with a handsome face set off by a well-trimmed goatee, Bogardus outshot all opponents in a number of local Midwest matches and once killed 500 passenger pigeons sprung from traps in a record 528 minutes—an impressive feat considering he used a muzzle-loading shotgun which he loaded

When the City of Saginaw returned from a hunt in Dawson, N.D. in 1889, nobody had to ask if the Michigan sportsmen had good luck. Club-owned railroad sports cars were popular before the automobile.

himself. Moving on to New York, which even then was the mecca for all showmen, he switched to the new breech-loader shotgun, which gave him a chance to show his speed and endurance as well as marksmanship. In an amazing demonstration before a packed house in Gillmore Gardens on Jan. 3, 1878, he set about to break 5,000 glass balls in 500 minutes, a feat no one had ever approached before. Beginning at 2:40 p.m. and using a half-dozen guns which he plunged periodically in ice water to cool, he shot continuously for 480 minutes, 15 seconds and broke 5,156 targets, an undisputed world record in skill and endurance. His name was soon a household word among the nation's sportsmen; and after he toured Europe, performed before royalty and outshot all challengers, he began calling himself the world's wing shot champion.

But everybody is after the champion, and out of the Far West at San Francisco came a loud challenge to Bogardus. Tall, six-foot-two Dr. W. F. Carver, with long flowing hair and a red mustache, offered to meet Bogardus head-on in a number of matches with substantial side bets. The self-taught dentist had also learned his craft by market hunting, but, unlike the Midwesterner, Carver killed buffalo for the Union Pacific Railroad crews. He boasted he could shoot more glass balls, either afoot or horseback, or kill more buffalo "and, if they were not to be found, elk" than the world's champion. Astoundingly, he would do it not with a shotgun, but with a *rifle*.

Few took his challenges seriously, as he was unknown in the East, but on July 13, 1878, before an incredulous crowd and using six Winchster rifles, he broke 5,500 glass balls in 420 minutes to better Bogardus' record with a shotgun. The stage was set for a much publicized and ballyhooed match in which the two would shoot 20,000 glass balls for the title, but the match never took place, as each shooter apparently preferred to stage his own exhibitions.

Then in 1884, another Midwestern sharpshooter caught the attention of the public. No manly bearing or titles had petite, 100-pound Annie Oakley. She came from a poor family and, unlike the market hunters, learned to shoot by practicing on the woodlot rabbits and squirrels. But with either a shotgun or rifle she was equally deadly. After outshooting all opponents in local matches for accuracy, she and her husband Frank joined Buffalo Bill's Wild West Show in 1885. Here, she caught the fancy of the public by demonstrating her accuracy shooting ashes off the cigars of smoking patrons, sometimes the cigars themselves, or a penny held by her husband, or the exact centers of playing cards in a demonstration of rapid fire. She took on all challengers here and abroad and usually outshot them. It was no idle boast that anything they could do, she could do better. Such was the fascination with the Ohio farm girl that, when she died in 1926, she was mourned throughout Europe and the United States. Even a half century later, Annie Oakley is the best-known shooter in American history.

It was not by accident that Bogardus and the other popular shooting heroes turned from killing live pigeons to breaking glass balls in the 1880s. Despite the large nestings of these birds and their seemingly unlimited numbers, it became harder for market hunters to meet the demand. We know now that the decade of the 1880s was the last to see the passenger pigeon in sizable flocks; by the turn of the century, the species was all but gone. Few, if any, contemporaries dreamed the pigeon would soon be extinct, yet there was growing popular clamor to stop using captured live birds for target practice. Moreover, sportsmen's clubs began to think of themselves as protectors of wildlife against the commercial market hunters. Most thoughtful sportsmen were embarrassed and disgusted when the New York Association for the Protection of Fish and Game held its annual meeting at Coney Island, N.Y. in June, 1881 and in a nine-day trapshooting contest killed 20,000 pigeons, many too ill or too young to fly out of the traps.

In 1875, a group of men representing 10 local clubs in Michigan met in Grand Rapids to form the first statewide Michigan Sportsmen's Association. Unlike most state groups of the day, the MSA was not a social gathering or a means to find the top trapshooter in Michigan, but was dedicated to high principles of wildlife conservation. In its constitution, the members clearly set forth their objectives:

"This association is organized for the purpose of securing the enactment of judicious and effective laws for the protection, at proper times, of wild game of fur, fin and feather whose flesh affords nutritious food and the pursuit of which furnishes a healthful recreation, and also all the birds that assist the agriculturalist and the horticulturalist in the protection of their crops, by the destruction of noxious animals and insects, and the enforcement of all laws for such purposes."

The association was fortunate in attracting a number of individuals who were to make outstanding contributions to its work. In 1876, the year after its founding, Dr. Ezra S. Holmes of Grand Rapids was elected president. His good sense and abilities were responsible for keeping the organization on a high intellectual plane so that no one should doubt its serious purposes or claim it to be merely another social club. Henry B. Roney of East Saginaw, who served as secretary during the early years, was to have much to do with the success of the campaign against market hunting. Cyrus W. Higby of Jackson was to perform the important function of acting as the group's first state "game warden." William B. Mershon of Saginaw was ultimately to be distinguished not only as one of the state's leading sportsmen, but as one who until his death in 1943 consistently fought for better wildlife conservation. He was elected secretary of the association in 1881 and held the office a number of years.

The goals of the organized sportsmen reflected, of course, their concept that wildlife should be used primarily for recreation. Although this concept seemed obvious to them, they soon found it hard to change the traditional view that wildlife existed mainly to supply men with food. Beginning in 1875, they urged the Legislature to ban commercial hunting in Michigan for out-of-state markets, but found only limited support in Lansing. Most legislators were either indifferent to the extent of market hunting or concerned over the constitutional question of whether a state could reserve wildlife for its own citizens. While they could not do much about the latter, they urged Henry Roney to research the former and report to the association. His was to be the first scientific attempt to determine the use made of the state's wildlife resources.

Sensitive, mild-mannered Henry Roney was probably the least likely candidate to enter the uncontrolled and often violent world of the 19th century market hunter. He taught violin to children in East Saginaw and with his neighbor, Mershon, represented the county sportsmen in the MSA. In an age when many sport hunters measured their success in numbers of deer killed, Roney quietly stalked his game in the woods north of Bay City "in season" and felt that the hunt, rather than the meat, was important. He was not particularly vocal during the MSA sessions, but game hogs and professional market hunters infuriated him, and he willingly accepted President Holmes' assignment to gather hard data on the extent of commerical hunting in Michigan.

Roney soon found that determining the extent of deer killed in the state in 1877 was not easy. There was no state agency keeping game records. Indeed, other than a few laws that were not enforced and a Fish Commission that was trying only to restock the Great Lakes with whitefish, Michigan had no game conservation in any form. Market hunters gave no interviews, railroad company records were not public information, and most people were either indifferent to commercial hunting or supported it for the revenue it brought the community. Yet slowly Roney began to accumulate useful information from the sources available to him.

Roney corresponded with sportsmen in southern Michigan who, like him, hunted in the north along the new railroad tracks. He asked for numbers of deer they killed and what they observed happening in the woods. He traveled the Jackson, Lansing and Saginaw, the Flint and Pere Marquette and the Grand Rapids and Indiana lines not as a sportsman but as an observer during the summer and fall when most deer were killed, and in towns and villages he talked to local residents about deer. Through influential businessmen, he persuaded the railroads to show him shipping receipts for most stations of the Jackson Railroad from Pinconning in the south to its then terminus at Gaylord in the north. He clipped newspaper accounts which spoke of the success of hunting parties and related market hunting industries.

By the time the MSA held its annual meeting in 1881, Roney was ready with his report. Although he admitted his claim of 70,000 deer killed in 1880 was an estimate, he supplied enough specifics to impress the assembled sportsmen with its reasonable accuracy.

The professional hunter operated without restraint in Michigan. The *Ogemaw Herald* reported a party of five killed

Two giants in the history of conservation in Michigan were William B. Mershon (above) and Chase Osborn (right).

31

The transformation of the forest by its first mantle of white always gave a peculiar exhiliration to hunts. Shown here with two bucks brought in to a camp on Whitefish Lake in Alger County are (from left) Charles Hebard of Philadelphia; Dean Williams of Marquette, who later became Episcopal bishop of northern Michigan, and B. F. Charlton of Marquette.

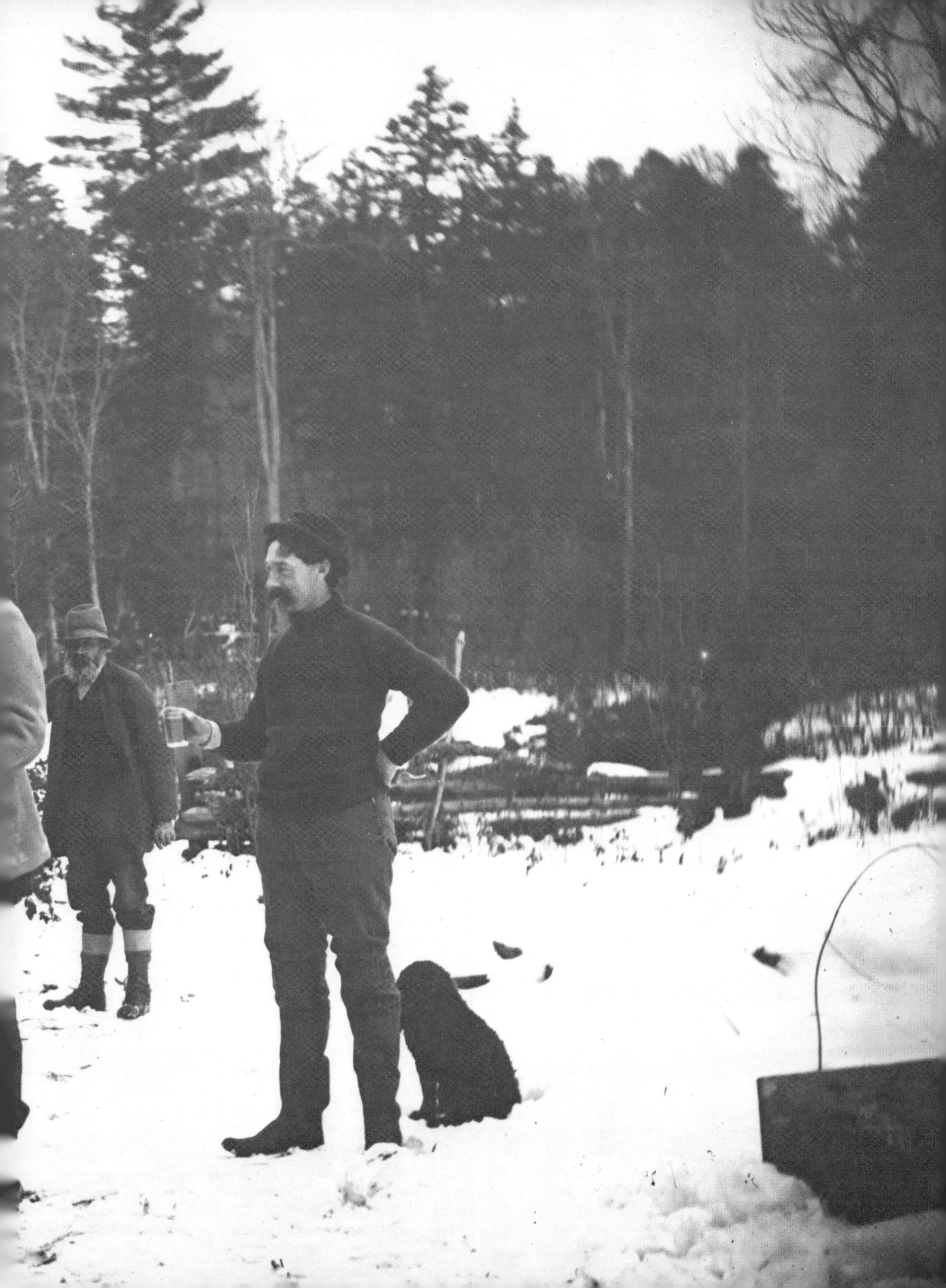

By 1900, many hunting camps were enjoying the comforts of home. The man second from left is holding a bottle of Schlitz beer.

34 deer, but Dick Parrish of Roscommon alone killed 81 for nonlocal markets. Eugene and James Atherton earned $650 for providing 156 deer in the 1880 season. Perhaps Chase Benjamin of Alpena could rank with Buffalo Bill, his contemporary, as he claimed to have killed 2,468 deer in his 29 years of market hunting. The editor of the *Bay City Tribune* told Roney that had he known the Saginaw sportsman was interested in market hunters, he "could have clipped enough from the northern exchanges to write a book."

Most of the deer killed were not for local use but for out-of-state. "It is a well-known fact," he said, to every traveler from the north during the hunting season that the JL&S railroad has to attach extra frieght cars to carry tons of deer carcasses. Station master receipts showed the poundage of venison shipped ranged from 12,500 at Pinconning to a quarter of a million at Roscommon.

Roney found that many deer were killed for their hides. Hunters found a market at every railroad station which brought them from $1 to $3 per hide. One East Saginaw buyer alone had received 4,500 hides during the 1879-80 season. Roney quoted a *Detroit Evening News* story reporting that the Blackburn Company had purchased machinery to make gloves and mittens at Alpena, "where deerskins are cheap and plenty all year."

The Saginaw sportsman concluded his report on the deer kill with some concrete recommendations. If this popular game animal was not to be completely wiped out, Michigan would have to stop furnishing the markets of the country with venison. This meant laws prohibiting its export. Deer could still be killed for use as food in Michigan, but the rail transport and sale of game should be allowed only a few days after the season ended.

Michigan should also prohibit the sale of red or spotted deer pelts, which, Roney believed, would end the insidious market in deer hides.

Roney then turned his attention to the market hunting of passenger pigeons. As we have already noted, the hunting of the migratory passenger pigeon goes deep into Michigan history. The arrival of these sleek transients each spring was greeted with considerable anticipation, and, if they nested in the neighborhood, every able-bodied person joined in the harvest. Nineteenth century settlers who were not usually emotionally moved by the forces of nature often took pen in hand to describe a flight of these remarkable birds.

It was not their beautiful red and blue plumage or their swiftness in flight or their foraging for food a hundred miles from their nesting or even their succulent taste in a pigeon pot pie that made the passenger pigeon awesome. It was their incredible numbers! A flight of these birds was a wonder to behold. Starting with an advance flock high overhead, there followed thousands of wildly chirping pigeons, and finally the main body which numbered in the millions. As they passed overhead at speeds of 70 miles an hour, they blotted out the sun as if it were night for hours at a time. John Audubon, who looked at a lot of birds in his time and was not given to overstatement, estimated one flock he saw at 1¼ billion birds. They were the most numerous of any species of North American wildlife.

In winter, the pigeons were found in the southeastern states, but as soon as the calendar said spring, most flew to nesting grounds in the hardwood forests of the Upper Midwest. By the 1870s, they were being killed for food and captured live for target use by trapshooting sportsmen's clubs. In 1878, circumstances were right for the biggest single slaughter of a wildlife species in American history.

In the dawn's early light of April 1, the first wave of birds appeared not much over treetop level east of the small sleeping northern village of Petoskey. They skirted Little Traverse Bay and headed northeast until they reached the shores of Crooked Lake near present-day Oden, 12 miles from Petoskey. After circling briefly, they settled down in the low hills in a beechwood forest. It was a natural choice with food and water close by, but if they had chosen to fly farther north toward the Straits of Mackinac or even west to the uninhabited Burt and Mullet Lake region, we probably would never have heard about them again. But by 1878, the Grand Rapids and Indiana Railroad had reached north of Petoskey, and the trackless wilderness of northern Michigan was no longer trackless. The nesting was within easy range of waiting markets, and, as fast as the telegraph could speak, every newspaper flashed the news that the pigeons were at Petoskey. On April 5, the *Grand Rapids Democrat* quoted Thomas Martin, a local meat dealer who had just returned from Petoskey, "There is no end to the pigeons in that locality."

By the time Martin returned to Crooked Lake a few days later, the nesting extended westward for miles and eventually covered an incredible area 10 miles wide and 40 miles long.

Each train brought market hunters and their equipment of nets, poles, guns, barrels and cash. They vied with each other to contract for local help from the townspeople and farmers, as well as from a large Ottawa Indian community across the bay at present-day Harbor Springs. Wagons were leased or bought in a frantic race to harvest the birds before they moved to inaccessible areas. The Grand Rapids and Indiana put on additional cars to haul a continuous procession of barrels and crates of pigeons. Eventually, nearly 500 market hunters were aided in the hunt by over 2,000 local residents.

At the nesting grounds, activity was frenzied. Men moved through the groves with long, flat-ended poles, striking birds in flight and dislodging the young squabs from their nests. Some attacked the trees with axes and saws, and when the trees fell with a resounding crash, the young birds were gathered as they fluttered along the guano-covered ground. Teamsters maneuvered their flat-bed wagons as close to the edge of the woods as possible and, as soon as barrels of dead and dying pigeons were filled, rumbled down the forest road to Petoskey.

In the meantime, netters worked the clearings. Some baited the ground with wheat, oats, corn or wild nuts, while others stretched out a hundred-foot long net. They tied the leading edge to bent saplings which, when released, flew through the air in an arc, trapping dozens of the feeding birds beneath the net. To decoy the flying pigeons, other hunters lay in concealment and maneuvered, by strings, captured birds or "stool pigeons" tied to hinged perches, causing the birds to flap their wings wildly. When the trap net was sprung, scores of men and boys captured the live birds and jammed them into nearby crates. Rarely were guns fired in the nesting area because the large numbers not only made it a waste of gunpowder, but increased the danger the birds would fly away.

How many pigeons were killed in the Petoskey nesting of 1878? We will never know exactly because no one counted them. "Carload lots," reported the *Detroit Evening News*. "Six tons a day" went south, said the *Grand Traverse Herald*. Others reported 50 to 60 barrels a day, and on one Sunday alone,

Group of hunters gather to admire a fine buck in this 1901 photograph.

128 barrels, each filled with 360 dead birds, and 108 crates of live pigeons were shipped. The most conservative estimate made by market hunter and meat dealer Thomas Martin was that 1,500,000 birds were taken in the five months they nested at Petoskey in the spring and summer of 1878.

Roney had been one of the observers at the Petoskey nesting and gave an emotional account of the pigeon harvest as part of his indictment of market hunting. He had ridden the Grand Rapids and Indiana north, watched pigeoneers net and kill the flying birds, but the sight in the nesting grounds sickened him. Everywhere he saw:

"A large force of Indians and boys at work, slashing down the timber and seizing the young birds as they fluttered from the nests. As soon as caught, the heads were parted from the tender bodies with the hand, and the dead birds tossed into heaps. Others knocked the young fledglings out of their nests with long poles, their weak and untried wings failing to carry them beyond the clutches of the assistant who with hands reeking with blood and feathers, tears off the head of the living bird and throws the quivering body on the heap."

The sportsman's attack on market hunting, and particularly his estimates of numbers killed, received considerable publicity. While most people accepted the fact that the passenger pigeon was probably being killed in record numbers, few seriously believed his estimate that not a million but a billion birds had been killed at Petoskey. Likely Roney threw out that figure only to offset a general apathy resulting from the widespread belief that the passenger pigeons were so numerous they needed no protection even in their nesting roosts. If he did not arouse the public, he did put the market hunters on the defensive for the first time.

Martin struck back at Roney. His rebuttal, which appeared in the Jan. 25, 1879 issue of *American Field,* argued that pigeons, although wild, were simply an article of commerce like "corn, hogs, beeves or sheep." There was no difference between killing them in Petoskey or the Chicago stockyards.

Moreover, market hunters contributed to the local economy because they left $35,000 "in good greenbacks right among the most needy of these people," who were struggling to make a living in a hostile climate. To protect the pigeons entirely, he warned, you would have northern Michigan overrun with a pest that would destroy the farmers' seed as fast as sown. As long as the forests remain and food is plentiful, the pigeon will survive, he concluded. "The pigeon is migratory and it can take care of itself."

Of course, Martin was wrong. The pigeons needed protection, but it came too late. Neither Roney nor anyone else foresaw the amazing decline in the species that occurred soon after Petoskey. Within a few years, flocks returning north in the spring were small, and by the late 1880s, they were rare. By 1900, the wild pigeons were probably gone. In 1914, "Martha," the last of her kind, died in a Cincinnati zoo just a generation after the great nesting in northern Michigan.

The lesson of the passenger pigeons was painful and permanent. In the history of wildlife conservation the story of this remarkable bird looms large. During the 70s, few spoke of "endangered species," and surely no one in his right mind would apply the phrase to the passenger pigeon. But, of course, it is the irony of abundance and extinction that makes this record of man's inhumanity to wildlife so tragic. It is probable

Marksman in this scene from the 1870s is shown shooting wild pigeons released from traps.

that the pigeons were doomed when the frontier ended in Michigan, but the fact remains not one single step was taken by the government to give even minimum protection until it was too late. The only passenger pigeons almost anyone living here today has seen are those few mounted on their perches in the natural history museums of Michigan State University and the University of Michigan.

The 19th century conservation laws were written by or for sportsmen and reflect their views. In reading the reminiscences of these sportsmen and looking at their photographs, it becomes obvious one measure of their success was number killed. Mershon himself recognized this when he wrote in 1923 that the pictures suggest "game hoggishness," but he justified it as simply a sign of the times. With few hunters in the field and quantities of game seemingly unlimited, it was an understandable view. The game was there to be used for food or recreation or, ideally, both. In attacking the market hunter, the sportsmen were concerned, not with killing wildlife *per se,* but with a systematic slaughter without regard to natural propagation, a practice they believed would soon wipe out the species they hunted for sport.

The first wildlife conservation law in Michigan gave protection to certain birds and animals for part of the year. In 1859, the

George Shiras III © National Geographic Society

Extraordinary size attained by whitetails in parts of northern Michigan is very evident in the above photograph taken in the 1880s, at the Shiras camp near the Whitefish River in Alger County. The successful hunter is A. O. Jopling of Marquette. Carcasses of deer at left were awaiting shipment south on the Michigan Central and the Grand Rapids & Indiana Railways at Mackinaw City.

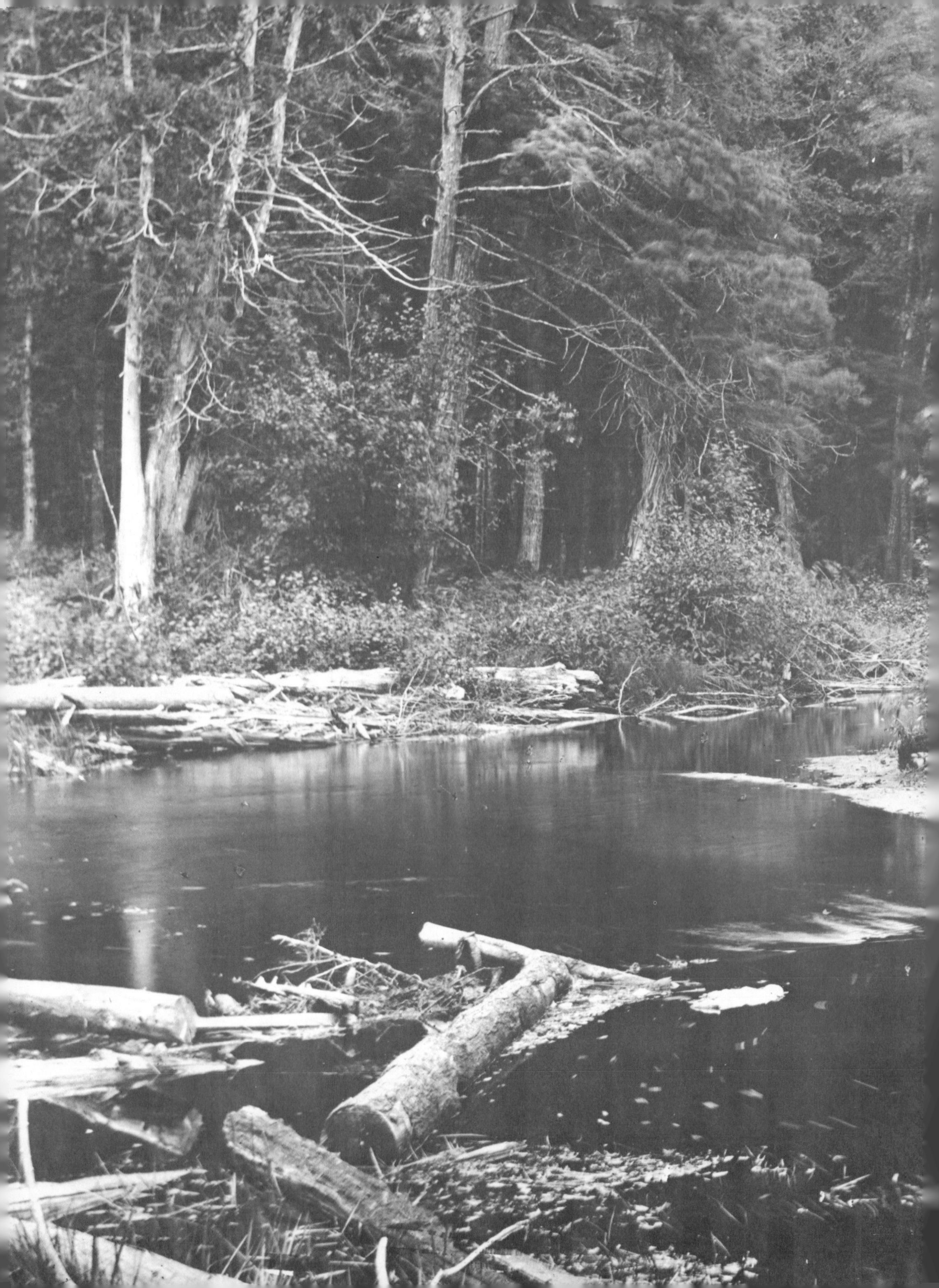

George Shiras III, naturalist, conservationist, sportsman and father of wildlife photography, brings two large bucks he shot back to camp in a skiff on Whitefish River. Photo was taken in the late 1800s.

George Shiras III © National Geographic Society

First good tracking snows helped fill game pole at Whitefish Lake Camp.

state forbade killing deer, turkey, woodcock, ruffed grouse, pheasants, "any partridge," duck and quail during certain months. Later amendments beginning in 1863 extended protection to geese, swans and beaver. Since then, hardly a year has passed without additions to the list or changes in the time of protection. Eventually, some species were given complete protection for aesthetic or other reasons, but historically wildlife has been considered a harvestable resource.

Secondly, the early laws, beginning in 1863, forbade the use of highly destructive weapons in killing game. Michigan pioneered in outlawing the cannon-like punt gun which was widely used for shooting waterfowl. Later acts prohibited snaring, deadfall, netting, shining for deer and other "unsportsmanlike" devices and methods. But in some cases, the hunters were given protection from their fellow hunters. For example, the law forbidding firing a gun in a passenger pigeon nesting ground insured the birds would not be frightened away by the noise, and the harvesters could do their work.

The third basic principle in Michigan's conservation history was the restriction on killing certain wildlife for commercial purposes. As early as 1869, the law loosely regulated the sale and transportation of protected game, but it was not until 1881, thanks largely to Roney's research, that market hunting was greatly curtailed. At that time, the state forbade the possession of deer, ruffed grouse, quail, prairie chicken and turkey, except for consumption as food within the state, and prohibited its transportation beyond the state after the legal hunting season. Later acts added other wildlife species to the list and tightened loopholes, but the 1881 act insured the use of game birds and animals primarily for sport and not for pot.

It was not easy for the 19th century sportsmen to get these basic conservation laws. Most people were apathetic or scornful of their attempts so long as wildlife seemed inexhaustible. However, the hunters were men of wealth and prestige in their communities and could put political pressure on the state's lawmakers far beyond their actual numbers. They lobbied intensely when the Legislature met in Lansing and were not afraid to spend money in promoting the cause of wildlife conservation. But as tough as their job was in getting the game laws on the statutes, it was nothing compared with the problem of enforcing those laws.

Under the constitution of Michigan at that time, the enforcement of state laws, such as game laws, was entirely a responsibility of the county sheriff and local prosecutor. In demanding enforcement of the game laws, sportsmen always carefully distinguished between the "poor homesteader," who killed for food and whose infraction of the law was presumably not so serious, and the "idle, lawless, ignorant" game law violators who killed deer and waterfowl for money. But this distinction was not apparent to most northerners. Local county prosecutors found it politically unwise to enforce the state laws against their constituents who killed "local wildlife," so charges had to be brought by outsiders, which was usually a futile exercise. In one celebrated case in Clare County, the violation was obvious, but the punishment did not fit the crime.

Early in the morning of June 10, 1881, August H. Mershon, father of William, was strolling down main street in Harrison when a wagon with two men and a freshly killed deer passed by. He noticed they were carrying a boat, gun and reflecting lantern, which indicated to him that they had just returned from a night of shining for deer. While he observed from a distance, the men carried the deer into John Hatfield's saloon, dressed it and distributed the venison to several stores down the street. After discussing the apparent game law violation with

These timber wolves were killed near Whitefish Lake in Alger County.

other members of the Saginaw Sportsmen's Club, Mershon pressed charges against the men.

The case seemed strong, but the sportsmen were in hostile territory and nothing went right. The county prosecutor obviously did not relish trying a case involving local people on a violation of a game law prohibiting shooting deer out of season which few Clare County residents took seriously. Witnesses who, with Mershon, had seen the circumstantial evidence of shining, suddenly refused to testify, and the faces of the jurists were not encouraging to the prosecution.

After a short deliberation, the jury rendered a verdict of "not guilty." When the amazed plaintiffs asked for an accounting, they were told the prosecution "never proved it was wild—it might have been a tame deer."

The elder Mershon was completely disillusioned by this experience. "I am satisfied," he said, "that no jury can be impaneled in the ordinary way, by the officers now in charge, no matter how direct the evidence and positive the testimony."

Moreover, he believed violations were so widespread that few local residents would take it upon themselves to initiate prosecutions. In forwarding to the Michigan Sportsmen's Association his father's report of this incident, William B. Mershon added the comment, "Please remember, gentlemen, these violations are not made by the settler and the homesteader, but by a lawless set of idle, whiskey-drinking bums."

It was not the last time the state sportsmen were frustrated by adverse local sentiment in their zeal to uphold the conservation laws. The defendants may have been idle, whiskey-drinking bums, but the residents of Harrison resented outsiders in the person of idle, whiskey-drinking, rich sportsmen coming to try to put them in jail.

After the fiasco in Clare County, the sportsmen, through the MSA, tried to enforce the game laws by establishing a club game warden. In 1882, Cyrus Higby of Jackson was appointed "state association protective agent" to organize sportsmen's clubs in northern Michigan and "especially see that the laws were enforced by moral suasion when possible, by vigorous prosecution when necessary." In this way, they hoped to get around the lack of enthusiasm of the local prosecutors for game law enforcement.

At Bay City in 1880, the sportsmen passed a resolution stating if there were "a better understanding on the part of the actual settlers of the *spirit of humanity and generosity which activates the Association's efforts to perpetuate the natural and bountiful food supply of game,* there would be perfect harmony and cooperation between them." But the fact is this high sounding platitude had no effect in bringing about general support for the law.

When it came right down to it, the sportsmen and the northern residents had little in common. There was more to separate them than to bring them together. The affluent visitors from the city came to look upon the north as a vast hunting grounds where animals should be preserved for their sporting enjoyment. The settlers, while happy to sell food, provide transportation and guide service to their guests, considered them as outsiders, as migratory as the passenger pigeon, and certainly as having no business coming in and telling them what to do.

Higby's tenure was short-lived, partly because the MSA renewed its political lobbying efforts to get the state to enforce the laws. He did organize a few local clubs and tried hard to convince the nonsportsmen of the value of protecting wildlife. However, his major contribution was to publicize the need and demonstrate that the state's organized hunters were willing to finance enforcement out of their own pockets.

Finally in 1887, after years of agitation, the State of Michigan accepted the principle of state, rather than local prosecution when the Legislature created the office of state game warden.

During the late 19th century, the sportsmen also struck hard at what they considered unsportsmanlike hunting on the sabbath. They were particularly annoyed by a class of hunters from the cities who would go out on Sunday in a steady procession carrying "everything from a flintlock to a breech loader and shoot at everything that gets up before them whether in season or not."

The native American of low income who worked six days a week and could ill afford to take time off to hunt naturally would be affected by a law prohibiting Sunday hunting, but the sportsmen were also taking aim at the increasing numbers of Old World immigrants who did not share the concept of the "fair hunt." Despite support from the religious community, they were never able to ban Sunday hunting, although both Ohio and Indiana had such a law.

From the time the state began to enforce the game laws in 1887 until after World War I, there were significant economic and social changes in Michigan that greatly affected the hunter and the state's wildlife. Improvements in transportation, especially the spread of railroads, the advent of the bicycle and the automobile, brought a new surge of tourism and a wider use and pressure on game birds and animals. Increases in population in the south and the spread of towns and villages northward meant more hunters had to share less hunting land. And as the demand for more wildlife protection increased, so did the cost, and new ways of paying for the services had to be found. With a more scientific approach to game management, as it came to be called, came the realization that habitat and other influences were more important than hunting restrictions in the conservation of wildlife.

The preservation of Michigan's forests is of such vital importance for wildlife that it is surprising little attention was given this problem until the late 1880s. Forest fires which swept across the state in the 1870s fed on the slashings left in the wake of the loggers, destroyed the natural cover of wildlife and exposed a sobering barrenness that fanned the faint embers of wildlife ground cover conservation. The first state forestry commission, headed by Charles W. Garfield of Grand Rapids, recommended a program of reforestation and tough burning regulations to prevent forest fires. In its report of 1888, Garfield quoted with approval a statement by Arthur Hill of Saginaw, a pioneer in reforestation, who said, "Although there are stringent laws for the protection of Game, the forests they lived in were neglected." It was the first official state recognition there was some connection between game and their habitat.

In 1900, the commission established the first state land reserves and began the first feeble efforts in replanting. They started on a few hundred acres in Roscommon and Crawford Counties that were "bad, miserable and burned over."
They first had to convince the local county supervisor the land could not grow wheat and potatoes. Later, as cut-over land reverted to the state for nonpayment of taxes, the state holdings increased tremendously in the northern counties. In the early years of the 20th century under Presidents Theodore Roosevelt and William Howard Taft, hundreds of thousands of acres of federal land in Michigan were withdrawn from sale and brought into a national forest system. Today, of course, most hunting in the north is done on those state and federal lands.

42

Forest fire can be both friend and foe of wildlife, depending on circumstances. Hunter in inset photo met his monstrous buck in 1910 season in second growth clearing where a forest fire had swept through not many years before.

A program to set aside private game refuge areas got under way by 1900. The idea was not new, and like many other conservation principles, it came from the sportsmen. President Holmes of the MSA read a paper in 1881 advocating a game preserve where quail would be protected through the winter. The Pere Marquette Fishing Club bought 17,000 acres in 1900 and strictly regulated hunting to increase numbers of wildlife. In 1904, Caribou Island in Lake Superior was purchased and converted into a game preserve by nine sportsmen, including Chase Osborn of Sault Ste. Marie. William B. Mershon, who hunted on the north branch of the Au Sable near Lovells, bought a large tract, regulated hunting and hired his own warden to enforce state laws.

The owners of these preserves made their own hunting and fishing regulations, which were frequently far ahead of state or federal laws. Mershon almost singlehandedly got the state to restrict fishing to flies only on that part of the Au Sable which ran through his preserve. At an 11,000-acre refuge in the eastern part of the Upper Peninsula at Munuscong, the sportsmen-owners prohibited spring shooting of waterfowl over nine years before a federal law made that sport illegal in Michigan. Some private preserves were created solely to give outright protection to wildlife, such as Henry Ford's 2,100-acre estate in Dearborn.

The state lagged behind these private efforts in game refuge conservation. Roney warned as early as 1878 that the subject of "game preserves in every state is one which ere long must be met and considered, or hunting for larger game will before many years become a luxury to be enjoyed only by the wealthy few whose time and means will permit them to take long journeys."

Several game wardens in the 90s urged the Legislature to set aside land, but it was not until 1913 when a wealthy Grayling lumberman, Rasmus Hansen, gave a 40,000-acre tract to Michigan for a game refuge that the program began on a state level. The act accepting Hansen's gift also provided any individual could give land to the state for refuge purposes and authorized the game warden to create game preserves on public lands. The following year, 55 parcels amounting to 25,000 acres were dedicated to the preservation of wildlife. Within a few years, over 650,000 acres were in the refuge program.

The most dramatic success along this line was the establishment of a federal game refuge and national park on Isle Royale, largely through the persistent efforts of Albert Stoll, the conservation editor of the *Detroit News*.

The purpose of the state game refuges was to provide a sanctuary for wildlife. Here, hunting would be restricted or entirely banned, and the game birds and animals would have a chance to propagate and increase in numbers. The privately-owned and operated preserves had the same objective, although the rules of hunting and the use of wildlife were set by club members.

As the pressure on domestic wildlife grew, some sportsmen experimented in introducing game birds and animals from abroad. As early as 1880, the old MSA talked about bringing the "gray partridge" to Michigan. About 1900, Mershon bought and released a small number of "mongolian pheasants" in the fields near his home, but without much luck. He noted wryly that "the taxidermists around Saginaw did a thriving business" in selling these mounted birds. In 1906, he had better luck with his experiments with Hungarian partridge. He imported 50 pair, which he set out in Saginaw and Clare Counties. For a number

In 1885, there were still some stands of virgin pine in northern Michigan like those pictured here. On opposite page, members of Turtle Lake Club near Alpena begin morning hunt for deer. Ex-Postmaster General Harry S. New, captain of the hunt, is in the lead and Francis McMath of Detroit is immediately behind him.

of years, he got favorable reports on them.

The Cleveland-Cliffs Iron Company, which owned Grand Island in Lake Superior, actively propagated blacktail deer, antelope and mountain sheep in 1905, but the western emigrants did not thrive.

These private attempts to populate the fields and woods with exotic foreign game birds and animals were experimental, unscientific and doomed to fail. However, far from losing their enthusiasm for the concept, the sportsmen tried to persuade the state to get into the business.

Although the early game wardens recognized the private efforts at game propagation and introduction of non-native species and urged the state to support them, it was not until 1913 that Michigan officially began this program. At the Hansen refuge near Grayling, German deer and wild turkeys were raised, the latter with such initial success that plans were made for a hunting season in the near future. In 1916, the state bought a 196-acre farm near Mason and soon began propagating golden and silver pheasants, wild ducks and even, at a cost of $125 each, reindeer from Norway.

Of all these efforts, by far the most successful was the work done with the Chinese ring-necked pheasant. These birds were first introduced in the United States privately in 1881 near Portland, Ore. and in 1895 in Ottawa County, Michigan as a substitute for the ruffed grouse, which had disappeared from the southern part of the state. Serious efforts to propagate and release did not begin until 1917, when 65 hens and 30 cocks were bought for the Mason farm. The following year, they increased to 950, and in 1918, thousands of birds were released throughout southern Michigan. So well adapted did they become that in 1921 the state allowed a fall hunting season, and shortly after the pheasant became the principal game bird in southern Michigan.

The 20th century hunter enjoyed the sport as much as his 19th century father, but he faced increasing regulations and restrictions of which his father never dreamed. After 1895, he could kill only five deer in a season and had to pay 50 cents for a license for the privilege. He could only possess 75 game birds and that, too, required a license in 1905. Many of his fellow sportsmen wanted to stop the spring shooting of all migratory waterfowl, but that was not to come until after World War I. If he was careless with his rifle and killed or wounded someone, he could go to jail for 10 years after 1903. And if all that was not bad enough, the Audubon Clubs and Humane Societies seemed to be springing up like mushrooms, and they sometimes sounded disturbingly anti-hunting.

Halting the spring shooting of migratory waterfowl stemmed from enactment by Congress of the Migratory Bird Treaty Act in 1918, one of the major landmarks in conservation legislation. The act gave the federal government the authority to set waterfowl seasons, bag limits and other regulations. It was written and introduced by a Michigan man, George Shiras 3rd of Marquette, while he was a member of Congress from 1903 to 1905 and received strong support from Theodore Roosevelt, Shiras' long-time sporting friend. Shiras, incidentally, is considered the father of wildlife photography, having pioneered in taking pictures of mammals and birds with crude photographic equipment in the vicinity of his hunting camp on Whitefish Lake in Alger County. His work is preserved in a two-volume classic published by the National Geographic Society under the title, "Hunting Wildlife with Camera and Flashlight."

Enforcement of game laws was not achieved by the appointment of a state warden in 1887. At that time, the

Father of wildlife photography, George Shiras III is shown in bow of hunting skiff in 1893 holding flashlight used in taking night photos of deer and other animals on shores of Whitefish Lake. Box on revolving table in bow holds two cameras. Jacklight used to locate game is on top of camera box. Shiras, pictured in inset portrait through courtesy of the Marquette County Historical Society, authored far-reaching bill to protect migratory birds while he was a member of Congress.

George Shiras III ©National Geographic Society

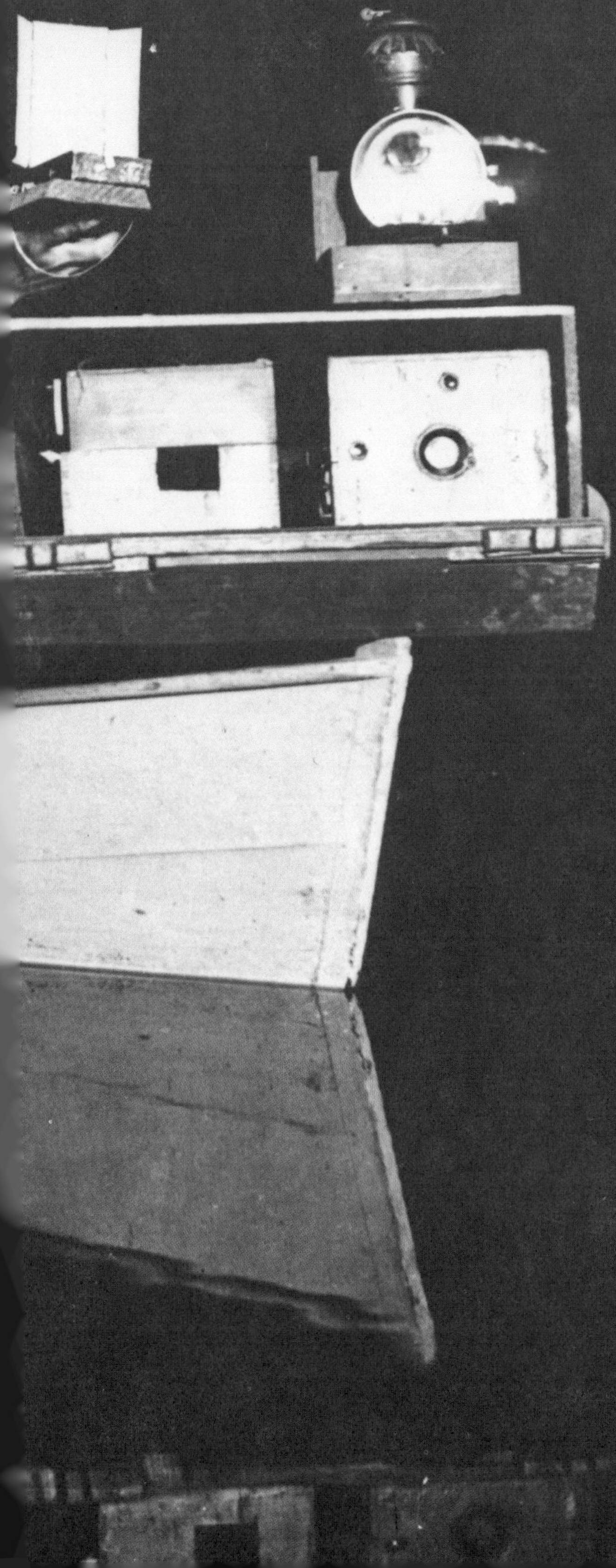

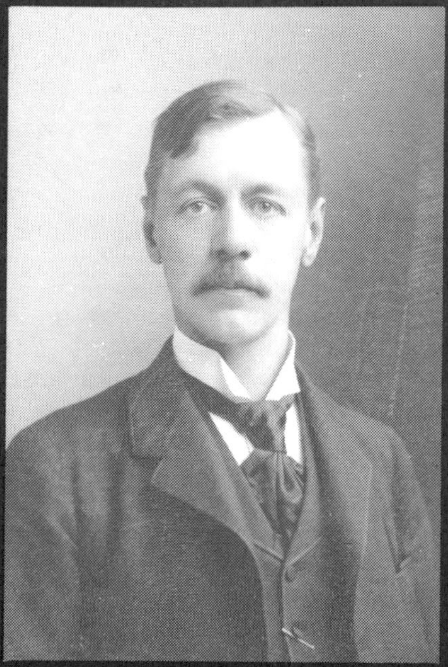

THE MICHIGAN SPORTSMAN

IN THE FIELD with the WARDENS

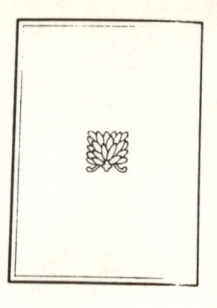

Violations and Prosecutions During June, 1922

COUNTY	COMPLAINT MADE BY DEPUTY WARDEN	VIOLATOR	FOR OFFENSE OF	FINE	COSTS
Alcona	John H. Speck	H. E. Kenaga	Possession of immature trout	$ 10.00	$ 3.50
Allegan	Stuart Agan	Frank Yates	Taking more than 10 black bass in one day	12.00	6.55
Allegan	Stuart Agan	August Geogesky	Having fish trap less than ½ mile from river	15.00	6.30
Allegan	Robert Hoy	Elmer Hogle	Catching undersized black bass and blue gills	8.00	7.70
Allegan	Robert Hoy	C. P. Coppock	Catching undersized black bass and blue gills	8.00	7.70
Allegan	Robert Hoy	Peter Korp	Obtaining license by false statement	18.00	6.30
Allegan	Robert Hoy	Albert Hastings	Catching undersized perch in Dumont Lake	3.00	4.90
Allegan	Robert Hoy	Ed. Beagle	Catching undersized perch in Dumont Lake	3.00	4.80
Allegan	Robert Hoy	Albert Streigel	Catching bass out of season in Dumont Lake	2.00	4.90
Allegan	Robert Hoy	Frank Streigel	Catching bass out of season in Dumont Lake	2.00	4.90
Allegan	Robert Hoy	Albert Meike	Catching bass out of season in Dumont Lake	2.00	4.90
Allegan	Robert Hoy	Ben Breuker	Catching blue gills out of season	1.00	4.90
Alpena	B. J. Napper	Joseph Toch	Fishing with spear and artificial light in inland waters	5.00	3.55
Alpena	B. J. Napper	Anthony Samp	Fishing with spear and artificial light in inland waters	5.00	3.55
Alpena	B. J. Napper	Theodore Hanson	Fishing with spear and artificial light in inland waters		
Alpena	B. J. Napper	Daniel Chaffee	Taking fish with a spear	Boy discharged on examination	
Alpena	B. J. Napper	Arlington Chaffee	Taking fish with a spear	Suspended	
Baraga	E. F. Sandberg	W. E. Pappe	Taking bass out of season	Pending	
Barry	Denner & Millenbacher	Will H. West	Taking blue gills in closed season	10.00	18.00
Barry	Ogden & Millenbacher	Fred Isaacison	Taking immature blue gills	....	5.50
Barry	Ogden & Millenbacher	Frank Rutter	Taking immature blue gills	5.00	5.10
Barry	Ogden & Millenbacher	Donald Lockwood	Taking immature blue gills	5.00	5.10
Barry	Ogden & Millenbacher	Will Sladek	Hunting without a license	10.00	4.95

In early 1920s, conservation law violators found their names in The Michigan Sportsman.

sportsmen had recommended the man be selected by them, but the act made it a political office. As a result, the game wardens from 1887 to 1921 were party faithfuls who used the office as a stepping stone for higher aspirations. Chase Osborn, who did a creditable job from 1895 to 1899 and who at least knew the difference between a blue jay and a ruffed grouse, went on to be railroad commissioner and later Governor. In fairness to the wardens, they had little money to work with as the state appropriation was only $1,200 in 1887 and went up very slowly. Between 1897 and 1908, when other functions besides enforcement were given to the department, the appropriation increased five-fold, but statewide convictions for all game law violations rose only from 400 to 500.

As we look back to that first decade of the 20th century, it seems the hunting sportsmen put too much stock in the need to enforce game laws vigorously, but it was their way to raise the status of wildlife conservation to a commendable state activity. During 1911, Mershon and his colleagues conducted their most intensive lobbying campaign since the 1880s to bring about political reform of the game warden's department. They wanted to remove the appointment of the warden and his deputies from the Governor and partisan politics and place the functions of wildlife matters in what they called an "honorary commission." This body, which could be appointed by the Governor, would choose a warden and his staff, and that choice would be based strictly on ability, dedication and scientific education. These employees would not be changed with a new administration, but would be under a civil service.

At first, the campaign seemed to go well. It was the height of the national reform movement. Theodore Roosevelt had given conservation a strong push at Washington, and Chase Osborn, a close friend of many sportsmen, was Governor. But the opposition was formidable, and the idea of job protection for wildlife personnel, when no other state employee had it, was ahead of the times. Then Game Warden Charles Pierce publicly opposed the idea because "I do not believe in any kind of civil service in regard to deputy game and fish wardens. The qualifications that a deputy needs are honesty, judgment and natural intelligence, and no possible examination can show these."

The bill passed the Senate, but was never voted on in the lower chamber, and when the session ended in 1911 without any change, the wildlife conservationists were dismayed and embittered. Mershon, who had hired a secretary and written countless letters to stir up support for the reform, admitted he was a "conservation crank," and in a letter to Gov. Osborn said, "I came to the conclusion last winter that I was out of tune with the people, that ninety-nine out of a hundred didn't care a cuss about saving or taking care of anything."

However, there was momentum for political reform, and significant changes in the state office concerned with game laws would take place in the next decade. In 1915, the game warden was made responsible to the Public Domain Commission, a land control agency, which removed it from the Governor's direct political patronage. Finally, as part of a major reorganization recommended by a study commission, all conservation activities of the state were grouped into a new Department of Conservation in 1921. Besides the game warden's office, these included the Board of Fish Commissioners, Forestry Commission, Public Domain Commission, Board of Geological Survey and the Michigan Parks Commission, which had just been created two years previously. The seven-man board was to be appointed by the Governor "with special reference to their training or

Early conservation officer examined deer kill at checking depot in northern Michigan.

experience along one or more of the principal activities" of the commission. Although intended as a sop to the sportsmen, the act left them suspicious by making the director of conservation the Governor's appointee.

To get support for their conservation program, the sportsmen increasingly promoted the process of public education. The nonsport hunting public would surely help if they only understood the need for protecting wildlife and recognized the relationship of birds and animals to their environment. With national attention focused on conservation during the Roosevelt era, schools of higher education, such as the University of Michigan and the Michigan Agricultural School, began to offer courses and later degrees in wildlife management. Public shows and exhibitions on birds and animals became popular, especially after photography and motion pictures became commonplace in the 20s. One such exhibition held in 1918 at the State Fair in Detroit was called the most ambitious program ever done by a state conservation agency by Game Warden John Baird, who added significantly that the department, "from its original status as a police patrol, . . . has evolved into an educational and 'more game' organization, and it now appeals more to the honor of the man who goes afield with the gun."

The 20th century hunter found getting to the game areas far simpler and more convenient than ever before. The railroads still solicited his business as they had in the 80s, and their growing network of tracks could take him to the farthest woods of the Upper Peninsula any day he wanted to go. But Henry Ford was to do even more. The automobile, when it ran right, was the ideal way to travel north, but sometimes getting there was more adventurous than the hunt.

Beginning in 1920, Gov. Alex Grosbeck dedicated his administration to building hard-surface roads that totalled over 2,000 miles in the next decade. During the prosperous 20s, many city workers began to get some vacation time and to head "up north" with gun, dog and tent in their Model T's. Of course, many oldtime hunters thought the sport was "going to hell" when these city folk began to appear in the woods, but their fears were unjustified. Most in this new wave of sportsmen not only developed a sensitiveness to conservation, but became the backbone of the many new sportsmen's clubs and state organizations. The Michigan Sportsmen's Association was revived in 1915 and succeeded by the powerful Michigan United Conservation Clubs (MUCC).

Organized in Owosso in 1937 to fight a threatened political takeover of the conservation movement, MUCC has grown to become the largest organization of its kind in the nation, with a membership of more than 100,000. The organization has been in the forefront of every important conservation battle in recent years and numbers among its principal accomplishments establishment of the state's public fishing site program, prevention of industrial development in the Porcupine Mountains Wilderness State Park, passage of a statewide bill banning throwaway beer and soft drink containers and successful lobbying for many pro-conservation measures in the Legislature. MUCC has engaged in a number of legal suits to protect the state's natural resources.

The population of Michigan increased by a million in the decade 1920 to 1930, which meant many more sportsmen to share the hunting grounds. Moreoever, the ease of travel brought out-of-state tourists to Michigan in greater numbers, and some came to hunt. In the decade, small game hunters doubled and the total number of deer licenses sold increased from 28,000 in 1921 to over 75,000 in 1930.

In recent years, the Department of Conservation largely

All from Burton Historical Collection

Former State Rep. Alonzo B. Green of Hillman (at left above) engages in congratulatory handshake with fellow hunter. Deer and Christmas tree are ready to be transported out of north woods. Appreciation for his setter's help shows in face of highly successful upland game hunter in photos above and below.

All from Burton Historical Collection

Buck kill on facing page was made in 1928 at the Lincoln Club adjoining the Turtle Lake Reserve in the northern Lower Peninsula. Members of the Turtle Lake Hunting Club are pictured below as they were about to depart for their runway stations in swamp adjacent to the clubhouse. Among those who hunted at Turtle Lake in 1928 was William B. Mershon, shown below on opposite page in his hunting garb.

determined the character of hunting in Michigan. The state not only has continued the traditional protection of wildlife species and enforcement of the game laws, but has used advances in animal and habitat technology as the basis for scientific game management. Recognizing the interrelationship of land and animals and the need to protect and regulate all aspects of the environment, the name of the agency was changed in 1969 to the Department of Natural Resources.

Continuing research is the basis for improved hunting. In some cases, longer seasons and increased bag limits have allowed a greater harvest while creating a healthier species in its changing habitat. Some game animals, for example, the white-tailed deer, have not only survived in heavily populated lower Michigan, but offer such good hunting that Mershon would be amazed. On the other hand, the government has increasingly restricted bag limits on some migratory waterfowl which show signs of depletion. As wildlife biologists learn more about these migrants, a greater burden is put on hunters who are required to distinguish between legal and illegal targets.

The department has continued and expanded its program of supplemental planting and introducing of new game birds. A recent "put and take" pheasant program provides good hunting of hatchery-reared birds in southern Michigan. Wild turkey transplants, which had foundered miserably in the past, now show considerable promise and, as we have seen, offer a real challenge to any bird hunter. Moreover, successful trap and release programs make it possible to expand greatly the hunting range for wild birds.

The private hunting perserves, which have alternately flourished and declined in Michigan, show signs of rejuvenation. While most of the shooting involves pheasants, some operators are experimenting with more exotic species. Convenience and guaranteed targets are appealing to some hunters who are willing to pay for the privilege of hunting on artificially stocked private lands.

If the state was working to bring about better hunting in a modern society, the hunters themselves were changing. In the first place, there were far more of them. In 1975, three quarters of a million deer hunters took to the woods, a ten-fold increase from 1930. Also, they were far more knowledgeable of hunting techniques, thanks to scientific literature in a multitude of popular magazines. Being better informed, they demanded through their local and state associations not only more game, but improved quality of hunting.

The modern hunter is mobile. Unlike Mershon and his friends, who moved laboriously by train and wagon to relatively near hunting grounds and remained stationary for two weeks, today's deer hunter drives over a network of paved roads to a comfortable motel or "roughs it" in a well-equipped recreational vehicle in the most remote areas of the state. He is within hours of prime hunting grounds and can make short trips without taking much time off work. The awkward communal tents, heavy clothing, hired camp cooks, wood stoves and locally supplied foodstuffs are largely gone. Today's sporting goods manufacturers arm him with powerful weapons and improved ammunition; dress him in lightweight, comfortable clothing and insulated boots; bed him down in sleeping bags and nylon tents; provide him sophisticated cooking equipment and dried foods; and, if he wants, he can carry it all on his back.

What does the future hold for hunting in Michigan? Recognizing the pitfalls of making any predictions in an activity that has changed substantially even in the last century, we can draw some conclusions from a study of the past.

Man has been hunting in Michigan for 11,000 years, but it has only been about the last 100 that he has been regulated. The first game laws recognized the need to protect certain hunted species to insure a steady supply and make possible a yearly harvest. Future hunters will face similar regulations although allowable harvests through hunting will be based on achieving a "balance" between wildlife, its habitat and climatic conditions to a much greater extent than in the past.

The old-time hunters were right in working for scientific and professional management of the state's wildlife. Future generations may not necessarily see more game, but through planting programs and new introductions, the quality of hunting should be better. But the hunter will have to vie for public lands with the nonhunter, and those lands will be increasingly expensive to acquire and to maintain. Moreover, hard decisions will have to be made by the state in situations where hunting and the development of other natural resources are incompatible. Hunting on private game preserves will grow, but the operators will face increasing public demand for humane treatment of birds and animals.

It was not long after the first game law became effective that the first violation occurred. In the future, hunting regulations, no matter how enlightened, are not always going to have the support of everyone. It was a frustrating and embittering experience for the sportsmen who lost the 1881 Harrison illegal deer killing case because of local prejudice and resentment against outsiders, but it was significant that the wiser ones among them recognized that it would be necessary to educate the opposition in the wisdom and necessity of the law. Future local residents who live in the hunting areas must be convinced it is to their advantage to support intelligent game management, and they will only be convinced through patient and careful explanation.

Finally, we have seen that the course of wildlife conservation was not far along before it became necessary to protect completely from the hunter's gun certain species. The lesson of the passenger pigeon is that sometimes this protection comes too late. Future endangered species will get a better break. But who is going to determine what is "endangered"? If the concept that "animals have rights, too" ever becomes prevalent, the hunter himself will be an endangered species, but by then presumably vegetarianism will be the law of the land.

Hunting is as old as man; only the purpose of hunting has changed. Today, as it has for generations, the sport brings joy and recreation to many. To say that hunting is wrong contradicts thousands of years of man's needs and beliefs. Unlike many other natural resources, the birds and animals of the fields and forests are renewable, and with intelligent management they can survive as long as man survives.

Food and plenty of it is a prime necessity in a deer hunter's life (below). Facing page: Pheasant hunting near West Branch, October 1933.

Conservation Pledge

I GIVE MY PLEDGE AS AN AMERICAN TO SAVE AND FAITHFULLY TO DEFEND FROM WASTE THE NATURAL RESOURCES OF MY COUNTRY— ITS AIR, SOIL, AND MINERALS, ITS FORESTS, WATERS, AND WILDLIFE

Both from Burton Historical Collection

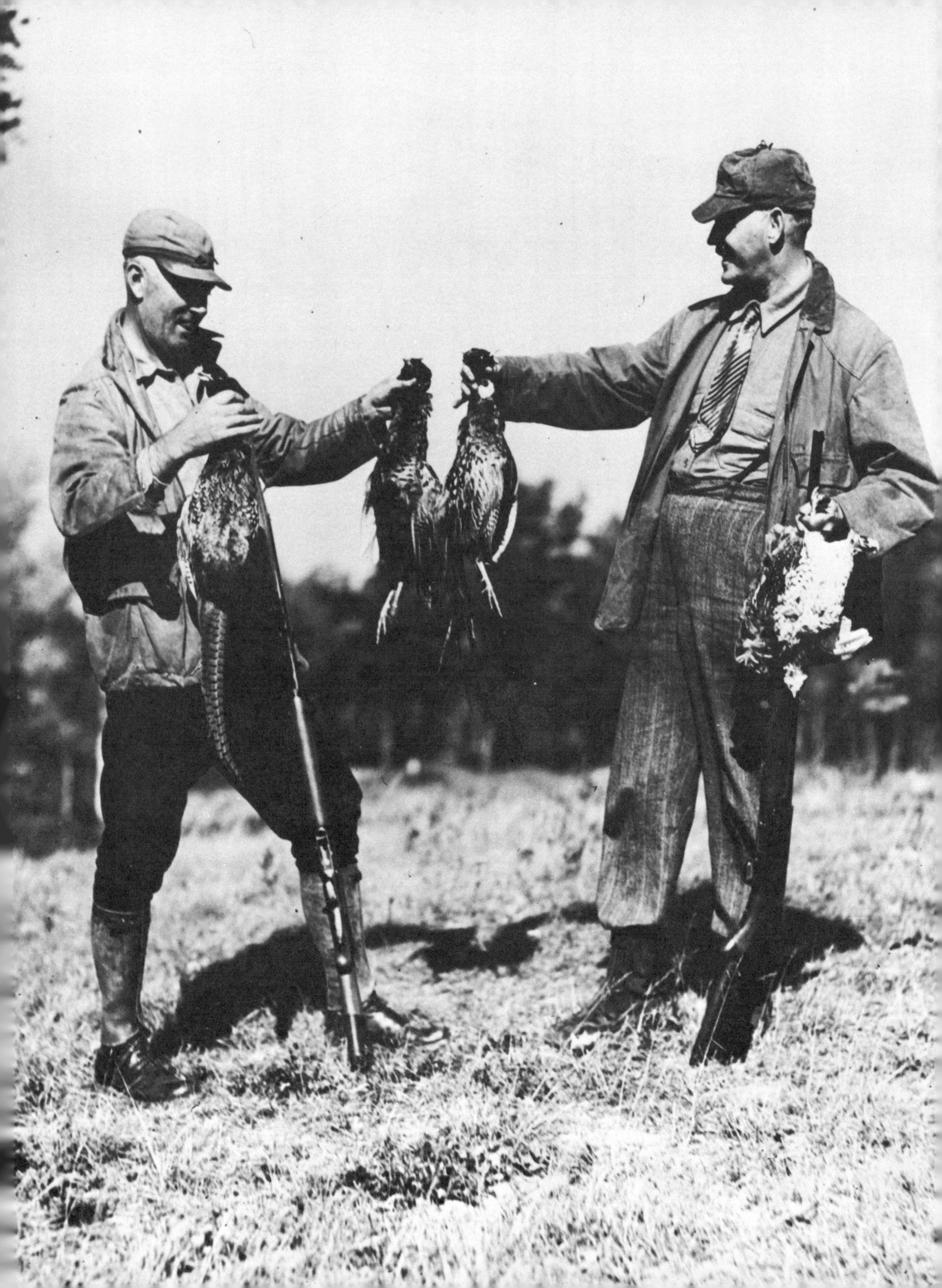

THE AUTHOR—Eugene T. Petersen is superintendent of the Mackinac Island State Park Commission. He was a Marine Corps officer in World War II and has taught history at the University of Detroit and the University of Michigan. His doctoral dissertation was entitled "History of Wildlife Conservation in Michigan."

MUCC is the Michigan United Conservation Clubs, a statewide organization dedicated to further and advance the cause of the environment and conservation in all phases and to promote programs designed to educate citizens in natural resource conservation and environmental protection and enhancement.

WILDLIFE CHEF

New revised edition features more than 300 recipes for preparing fish and game. Durable enamel cover.

Handy 6 x 9 inch size
107 pages—illustrated

$3.95

Order from MUCC P.O. Box 30235, Lansing, MI 48909

A Michigan magazine
for the Michigan sportsman...

Michigan OUT-OF-DOORS
December 1977
$1

1 year $9.00   2 years $15.00
order from MUCC P.O. Box 30235, Lansing, MI 48909